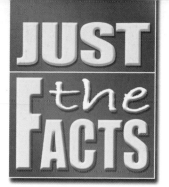

PREHISTORIC
WORLD

School Specialty Publishing

This edition published in the United States in 2006 by School Specialty Publishing, a member of the School Specialty Family. Copyright © ticktock Entertainment Ltd 2005 First published in Great Britain in 2005 by ticktock Media Ltd. Printed in China.

Library of Congress-in-Publication Data is on file with the publisher.

Send all inquiries to:
School Specialty Publishing
8720 Orion Place
Columbus, OH 43240-2111

ISBN 0-7696-4258-6

1 2 3 4 5 6 7 8 9 10 TTM 11 10 09 08 07 06

CONTENTS

HOW TO USE THIS BOOK

JUST THE FACTS, PREHISTORIC WORLD is a quick and easy-to-use way to look up facts about dinosaurs, early reptiles, amphibians, and mammals. Every page is packed with names, statistics, and key pieces of information about the history of Earth. For fast access to just the facts, follow the tips on these pages.

TIMELINES
A breakdown of the names given to the different subdivisions of time.

BOX HEADINGS
Look for heading words linked to your research to guide you to the right fact box.

INTRODUCTION TO TOPIC

TWO QUICK WAYS TO FIND A FACT:

● Look at the detailed **CONTENTS** list on page 3 to find you topic of interest.

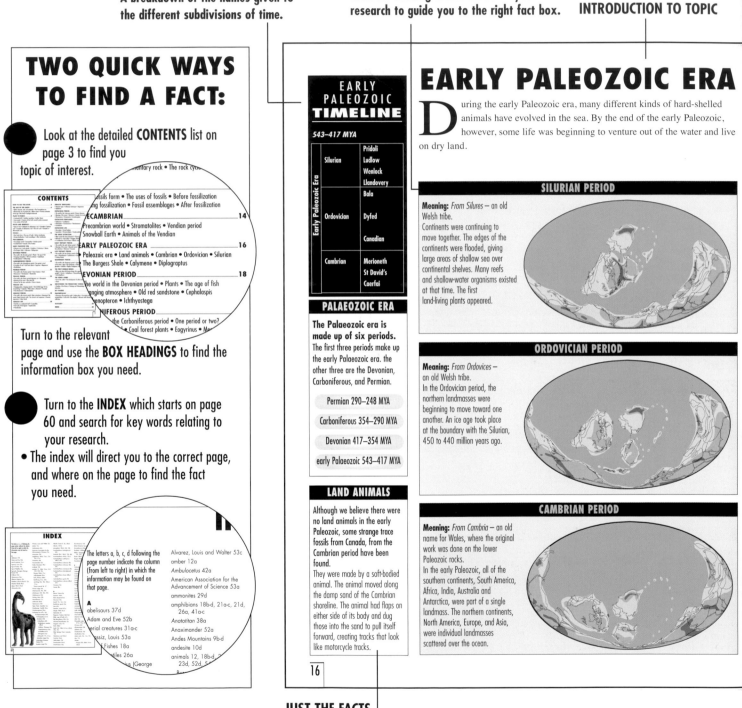

CONTENTS

...mentary rock • The rock cycle

...ssils form • The uses of fossils • Before fossilization
...ng fossilization • Fossil assemblages • After fossilization

PRECAMBRIAN 14
Precambrian world • Stromatolites • Vendian period
Snowball Earth • Animals of the Vendian

EARLY PALEOZOIC ERA 16
Paleozoic era • Land animals • Cambrian • Ordovician • Silurian
The Burgess Shale • Calymene • Diplograptus

DEVONIAN PERIOD 18
The world in the Devonian period • Plants • The age of fish
...nging atmosphere • Old red sandstone • Cephalaspis
...enopteron • Ichthyostega

...NIFEROUS PERIOD
...the Carboniferous period • One period or two?
... • Coal forest plants • Eogyrinus • M...

Turn to the relevant page and use the **BOX HEADINGS** to find the information box you need.

● Turn to the **INDEX** which starts on page 60 and search for key words relating to your research.
• The index will direct you to the correct page, and where on the page to find the fact you need.

INDEX

The letters a, b, c, d following the
page number indicate the column
(from left to right) in which the
information may be found on
that page.

A
abelisaurs 37d
Adam and Eve 52b
...erial creatures 31a-c
...ssis, Louis 53a
...d Fishes 18a
...tiles 26a
...us (George

Alvarez, Louis and Walter 53c
amber 12a
Ambulocetus 42a
American Association for the
  Advancement of Science 53a
ammonites 29d
amphibians 18b-d, 21a-c, 21d,
  26a, 41a-c
Anatotitan 38a
Anaximander 52a
Andes Mountains 9b-d
andesite 10d
animals 12, 18b-d, 2...
  23d, 52d, 5...
B...

EARLY PALEOZOIC TIMELINE

543–417 MYA

Early Paleozoic Era	Silurian	Pridoli
		Ludlow
		Wenlock
		Llandovery
	Ordovician	Bala
		Dyfed
		Canadian
	Cambrian	Merioneth
		St David's
		Caerfai

PALAEOZOIC ERA

The Palaeozoic era is made up of six periods. The first three periods make up the early Palaeozoic era, the other three are the Devonian, Carboniferous, and Permian.

Permian 290–248 MYA

Carboniferous 354–290 MYA

Devonian 417–354 MYA

early Paleozoic 543–417 MYA

LAND ANIMALS

Although we believe there were no land animals in the early Paleozoic, some strange trace fossils from Canada, from the Cambrian period have been found.
They were made by a soft-bodied animal. The animal moved along the damp sand of the Cambrian shoreline. The animal had flaps on either side of its body and dug those into the sand to pull itself forward, creating tracks that look like motorcycle tracks.

EARLY PALEOZOIC ERA

During the early Paleozoic era, many different kinds of hard-shelled animals have evolved in the sea. By the end of the early Paleozoic, however, some life was beginning to venture out of the water and live on dry land.

SILURIAN PERIOD

Meaning: *From Silures* — an old Welsh tribe.
Continents were continuing to move together. The edges of the continents were flooded, giving large areas of shallow sea over continental shelves. Many reefs and shallow-water organisms existed at that time. The first land-living plants appeared.

ORDOVICIAN PERIOD

Meaning: *From Ordovices* — an old Welsh tribe.
In the Ordovician period, the northern landmasses were beginning to move toward one another. An ice age took place at the boundary with the Silurian, 450 to 440 million years ago.

CAMBRIAN PERIOD

Meaning: *From Cambria* — an old name for Wales, where the original work was done on the lower Paleozoic rocks.
In the early Paleozoic, all of the southern continents, South America, Africa, India, Australia and Antarctica, were part of a single landmass. The northern continents, North America, Europe, and Asia, were individual landmasses scattered over the ocean.

JUST THE FACTS
Each topic box presents the facts you need in short, quick-to-read bullet points.

52–53 Uncovering the Prehistoric World Timeline

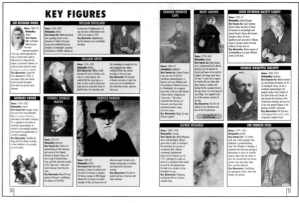

54–55 Key Figure Biographies

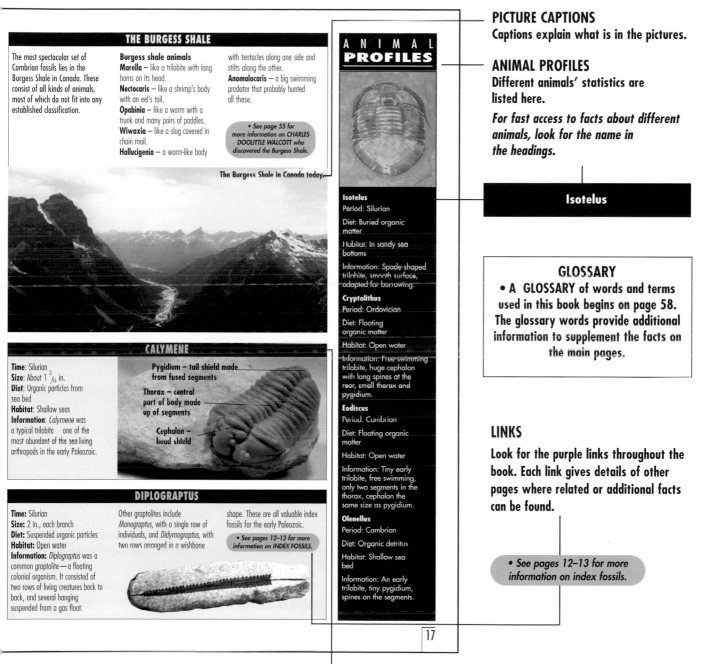

THE BURGESS SHALE

The most spectacular set of Cambrian fossils lies in the Burgess Shale in Canada. These consist of all kinds of animals, most of which do not fit into any established classification.

Burgess shale animals
Marella – like a trilobite with long horns on its head.
Nectocaris – like a shrimp's body with an eel's tail.
Opabinia – like a worm with a trunk and many pairs of paddles.
Wiwaxia – like a slug covered in chain mail.
Hallucigenia – a worm-like body

with tentacles along one side and stilts along the other.
Anomalocaris – a big swimming predator that probably hunted all these.

• See page 55 for more information on CHARLES DOOLITTLE WALCOTT who discovered the Burgess Shale.

The Burgess Shale in Canada today.

CALYMENE

Time: Silurian
Size: About 1 3/16 in.
Diet: Organic particles from sea bed
Habitat: Shallow seas
Information: *Calymene* was a typical trilobite – one of the most abundant of the sea living arthropods in the early Paleozoic.

Pygidium – tail shield made from fused segments
Thorax – central part of body made up of segments
Cephalon – head shield

DIPLOGRAPTUS

Time: Silurian
Size: 2 in., each branch
Diet: Suspended organic particles
Habitat: Open water
Information: *Diplograptus* was a common graptolite — a floating colonial organism. It consisted of two rows of living creatures back to back, and several hanging suspended from a gas float.

Other graptolites include *Monograptus*, with a single row of individuals, and *Didymograptus*, with two rows arranged in a wishbone

shape. These are all valuable index fossils for the early Paleozoic.

• See pages 12–13 for more information on INDEX FOSSILS.

ANIMAL PROFILES

Isotelus
Period: Silurian
Diet: Buried organic matter
Habitat: In sandy sea bottoms
Information: Spade-shaped trilobite, smooth surface, adapted for burrowing.

Cryptolithus
Period: Ordovician
Diet: Floating organic matter
Habitat: Open water
Information: Free-swimming trilobite, huge cephalon with long spines at the rear, small thorax and pygidium.

Eodiscus
Period: Cambrian
Diet: Floating organic matter
Habitat: Open water
Information: Tiny early trilobite, free swimming, only two segments in the thorax, cephalon the same size as pygidium.

Olenellus
Period: Cambrian
Diet: Organic detritus
Habitat: Shallow sea bed
Information: An early trilobite, tiny pygidium, spines on the segments.

17

PICTURE CAPTIONS

Captions explain what is in the pictures.

ANIMAL PROFILES

Different animals' statistics are listed here.

For fast access to facts about different animals, look for the name in the headings.

Isotelus

GLOSSARY
• A GLOSSARY of words and terms used in this book begins on page 58. The glossary words provide additional information to supplement the facts on the main pages.

LINKS

Look for the purple links throughout the book. Each link gives details of other pages where related or additional facts can be found.

• See pages 12–13 for more information on index fossils.

ANIMAL FEATURES

A more detailed study of an animal of the time. A picture accompanies the information to give a better idea of what life was like at that time.

THE PRECAMBRIAN EON 4,500–543 MYA

The Precambrian eon covers three eras and over 4,000 million years. However, during this period, primitive lifeforms were only starting to develop, and it wasn't until later that life truly began to take shape as we know it.

Proterozoic	2,500–543 MYA
Archaean	3,800–2,500 MYA
Hadean	4,500–3,800 MYA

This is what the surface of the Earth may have looked like whe it was still forming in the Hadean era.

THE AGE OF THE EARTH

The Earth is about 4.6 billion years old. During that time, there have been extreme changes in layout of the land and the oceans, as well as vast differences in the kinds of life that have walked on Earth's land, flew in its sky, and swam in its seas. While everything looks to be stable in our eyes, the Earth is constantly changing, continents are moving, and life continues to change.

Early Paleozoic 543–417	Devonian 417–354	Carboniferous 354–290	Permian 290–248	Triassic 248–206

First Signs of Life on Land
In the early Paleozoic period, life was predominantly sea-based. Hard-shelled animals were evolving at this time. By the end of the period, life was starting to venture onto the land.

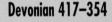

The First Reptiles
In the Carboniferous period, life on land was fully established. The coal forests are filled with giant insects and the first reptiles. The forests eventually formed the coal we use as fuel today.

The Reptiles Flourish
Between the Permian and Triassic periods, there was another mass extinction. This brought about a spurt in the development of lifeform. The first dinosaurs appeared on Earth.

The Age of Dinosaurs Begins
Dinosaurs evolved in the late Triassic period and ruled the Earth until the end of the Cretaceous period. As the continents moved apart, newer and more fantastic dinosaurs evolved on the separate continents.

HOW DO WE KNOW?

We can look at radioactive minerals in rocks.
Radioactive minerals change at a regular rate over time. By looking at the amount of radioactive mineral that has changed, we can figure out how long the changes have been going on, which provides the length of time since the mineral was formed.

OLDEST MINERALS, ROCKS, AND METEORITES

The oldest minerals – 4.3 billion years old. They were found in much younger sedimentary rocks in Australia.

The oldest rocks – 4.03 billion years old found in the Great Slave Lake in northwestern Canada (shown below). These are metamorphic rocks and are formed from rocks that already existed and must have been older.

The oldest meteorites – 4.6 billion years ago. They are assumed to have formed at the same time as Earth.

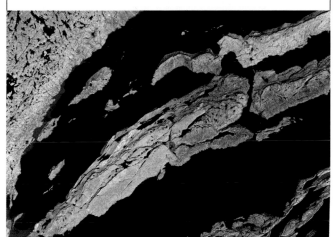

PREVIOUS ESTIMATES OF THE AGE OF THE EARTH

- **About 5 or 6 thousand years** – Going by the dates in the Bible and universally accepted until about 150 years ago.
- **25–40 million years – Lord Kelvin in 1862.** He based his calculation on how long the Earth would take to cool to its present temperature assuming that Earth began hot and molten. He did not know about radioactivity. Radioactivity continues to generate heat, so the Earth cools much more slowly.
- **Irish Geologist Samuel Haughton in 1878** suggested that the age could be estimated by measuring the depth of sedimentary rocks.
- **27.6 million years – Walcott in 1893.**
- **18.3 million years – Sollas in 1900.** Both he and Walcott were influenced by Haughton.
- **704 million years – Goodchild in 1897.**
- **96 million years – John Joly in 1889.** He was working on the rate of buildup of salt in the ocean.

Jurassic 206–144	Cretaceous 144–65	Tertiary 65–1.75	Quaternary 1.75–present

The Great Extinction
At the end of the Cretaceous period, a cataclysmic event occured that wiped out all the dinosaurs, pterosaurs, and sea reptiles. This cleared the way for the first mammals.

The Age of Mammals
After nearly all of life is wiped out by the Great Extinction, the Early Tertiary period sees life on Earth taking new direction. Gone are the dinosaurs and great pterosaurs that ruled the sky, new creatures that graze on the newly developing grass and plants thrive during this time.

Human Beings First Appear
Human beings first appeared about 200,000 years ago. Earth begins to look more and more like it does now.

PHANEROZOIC EON TO PRESENT DAY

The Phanerozoic eon covers three eras: the *Paleozoic*, highlighted in **GREEN**, the *Mesozoic*, highlighted in **PURPLE,** and the *Cenozoic*, highlighted in **RED**. Each one of these are then subdivided into different periods as noted. Although the Phanerozoic eon is only 543 million years, it covers the period when life advances on Earth.

GEOLOGICAL TIME SCALE

- When the geological time scale is shown vertically the oldest division is always at the bottom and the youngest, or the present day, is at the top.
- This reflects the sequence in which sedimentary rocks are laid down (see p10–11).

PLATE TECTONICS

In 1492, Christopher Columbus sailed across the Atlantic and became the first European recorded to have set foot in North America. His voyage took him 70 days. Today, the Atlantic Ocean is over 30 feet wider now than it was 500 years ago. The plate tectonics theory states that the Earth is made up of about 30 plates that sit on a layer of molten rock. the plates move about 4 inches a year. While that may not seem like a lot, combine that small amount with billions of years, and there is a large change.

CONTINENTAL DRIFT

Look at a map of the world. The shape of the east coast of South America fits into the west coast of Africa. People in the past have noticed this as well.

In 1620, Francis Bacon noticed the similarity but did not suggest a reason.

In 1668, P. Placet suggested that the Biblical Flood had forced the continents apart.

In 1855, Antonio Snider drew maps to illustrate how the world used

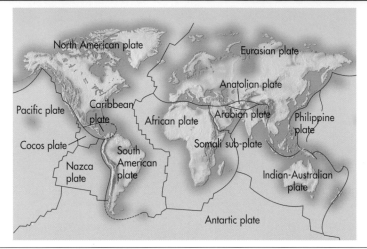

North American plate
Eurasian plate
Anatolian plate
Pacific plate
Caribbean plate
Arabian plate
Philippine plate
African plate
Cocos plate
Somali sub-plate
South American plate
Nazca plate
Indian-Australian plate
Antartic plate

to be, but nobody took him seriously.

In 1908, F.B. Taylor tried to explain it, along with the formation of mountains, by a movement of continents southwards from the North Pole.

In 1915, Alfred Wegener is credited with beginning the serious scientific discussion of the phenomenon.

• See page 55
ALFRED WEGENER.

SEAFLOOR SPREADING

- If the continents are moving apart, then something must be happening to the ocean floor between them. Scientists started discovering this during the late-20th century.

- The crew of the *US Atlantis,* in 1947, noticed that sediment was thin on the floor of the Atlantic Ocean. This meant that part of the ocean floor was younger than other parts.

- Various oceanographic surveys in the 1950s observed oceanic ridges, particularly the one in the middle of the Atlantic.

- American geologist Harry Hess noted in 1960 that the sediment was thinner over the ocean ridges than in the deeper waters at each side. The ridges were younger than the rest of the ocean.

- British geophysicists Fred Vine

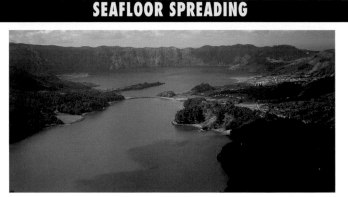

The Azores are a group of islands that lie on the Mid-Atlantic ridge, which were formed by molten rock as the plates move away from each other.

and Drummond Matthews found, in 1963, that the rocks of the ridges in the Atlantic Ocean were arranged in strips, magnetized in different directions. They had formed at different times when the Earth's magnetic field was pointing in different directions.

- Canadian geologist Lawrence Morley made the same observations in the Pacific Ocean in 1963.

- This showed that the oceans were growing larger at their ridges. Volcanic activity formed new seafloor there, and this moved away from the ridge as even newer material formed in between. Hess proposed the name *seafloor spreading*.

- Combined with *continental drift*, these two theories make up *plate tectonics*.

- The surface of the globe is made up of plates, like the panels of a soccer ball. Each plate is growing from a seam along one side and moving along beneath the next plate at the seam on the other side. The continents are carried by in these plates.

- As the continents move about, they occasionally crash into one another. This causes the edge to crumple up, forming mountains; fusing together to form bigger continents; or splitting apart as new seams grow beneath them.

- All the continents consist of ancient cores, that have been there for billions of years, and surrounded by progressively younger ranges of mountains.

ANOTHER THEORY

German geologist O.W. Hilgenberg and British physicist P.A.M .Dirac (in the 1930s) and British geologist H.G. Owen (in the 1960s) suggested that the continents were moving apart because the Earth was expanding. Few scientists accept this idea today.

SOME SPEEDS

- Movement of plates in North Atlantic — $^6/_8$ in per year. This is typical.

- Movement of plates in Pacific — $1\,^5/_8$ in per year. This is the fastest.

FEATURES OF THE EARTH CAUSED BY PLATE MOVEMENT

Aleutian Islands
Arc of islands formed where one ocean plate slides beneath another.

Mediterranean Sea
Where two plates are sliding next to one another, creating islands, mountains, and volcanoes.

Red Sea
Where the continent is already split.

Ural Mountains
The line along where two continents fused together in the distant past.

Andes
Mountains formed as an ocean plate is forced beneath a continental plate.

Mid-Atlantic Ridge
Where the two halves of the Atlantic Ocean are growing apart.

East African Rift Valley
Where a continent is beginning to split apart.

Australia
A continent being carried north as the plate moves.

Mariana Trench
Where one ocean plate is pushed up beneath another.

CROSS SECTION OF THE EARTH

Center — 3950 miles down.

Inner core — solid iron   upper boundary 3200 miles.

Outer core — liquid iron — upper boundary 1800 miles.

Mantle — mostly solid stone — upper boundary 3 to 6 miles beneath the ocean and 15 to 56 miles beneath the continents.

Crust — solid stone. The upper 60 miles of the crust and topmost mantle is called the *lithosphere,* forming the plates. The next 60 miles of the mantle is called the *asthenosphere,* which is the mobile layer on which the plates move.

ROCKS AND MINERALS

The crust of the Earth is made up of minerals. Usually, minerals form crystals of a particular shape, but sometimes these crystals are distorted or too small to see. When different minerals form together, the result is rock.

TYPES OF ROCK

There are three types of rock, and these form in different ways.

Igneous rock is formed when molten material from inside the Earth cools and solidifies. Usually the minerals can be seen as distinct crystals in igneous rock. There are two types of igneous rock:

1. Intrusive – formed under the surface of the Earth. This tends to be coarse with big crystals.

Intrusive rock

Extrusive rock

2. Extrusive – formed on the surface of the Earth from cooling molten lava. This is usually fine, with crystals that cannot be seen with the naked eye.

Sedimentary rock is formed from fragments that are laid down as layers. There are three types of sedimentary rock:

1. Clastic – formed from pieces of rock that have broken from rocks that already exist.

2. Biogenic – formed from material gathered by living things.

3. Chemical – formed as minerals crystallize out of seawater.

Metamorphic rock.is the result of existing rocks being heated and

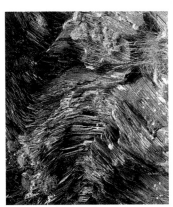

Metamorphic rock

Sedimentary rock

compressed by Earth's movements that cause their minerals to change. The original rock does not melt — otherwise the result would be an igneous rock. There are two types of metamorphic rock:

1. Thermal metamorphic – formed principally by the action of heat.

2. Regional metamorphic – formed principally by the action of pressure.

SEDIMENTS TO SEDIMENTARY ROCK

Sediments pile up in beds on the bottom of a river, sea, or lake, or even in a desert.

- The weight of the sediments on top compress those below.
- Ground water percolates through the beds, depositing minerals as it goes, cementing the sedimentary particles together.
- The result is a solid mass, called *sedimentary rock*.

In any undisturbed area, the oldest sedimentary bed is at the bottom, which is why it appears at the bottom of a geological time scale diagram.

EXAMPLES OF IGNEOUS ROCK

- **Granite** (intrusive) has big crystals created by cooling slowly. It is light in color because of the high proportion of silica in the minerals. It comes from deep in mountain ranges.

- **Gabbro** (intrusive) has big crystals. It is dark in color because of the low proportion of silica in the minerals. It is found deep in mountain ranges and the crust of the ocean.

- **Dolerite** (intrusive) is cooled near the surface, so it has smaller crystals that need to be seen with

a microscope.

- **Basalt** (extrusive) is very fine-grained due to rapid cooling. It is solidified lava flow. It has a black color because of the low proportion of silica minerals. It comes from freely-flowing volcanoes.

- **Andesite** (extrusive) It is very fine-grained due to rapid cooling. It is solidified lava flow. It has a pale color because of the high proportion of silica minerals. It is found in explosive volcanoes, such as Mount Saint Helens and Vesuvius.

Granite

EXAMPLES OF SEDIMENTARY ROCK

Conglomerate (clastic) is coarse, like a solidified pebble bed, and is formed from shingle beaches.

Sandstone (clastic) is medium-grained and formed from sand accumulated in river beds or deserts.

Shale (clastic) is fine-grained and formed from mud laid down in very thin beds in a river, lake, or sea.

Mudstone (clastic) is fine-grained like shale, but does not split into even beds.

Clay (clastic) is so fine-grained that it is difficult to see the fragments, even with a microscope. It is usually formed in still waters, such as lakes.

Coal (biogenic) is formed as vegetable material piles up in beds and does not rot away.

Halite/rock salt (chemical) is formed as salty waters dry out in lakes or sheltered bays.

Limestone can be clastic, from previously-formed limestone; biogenic, from seashells or coral reefs; or chemical, from dissolved calcite in sea water.

Sedimentary rocks are important for fossil formation.

Conglomerate

THE ROCK CYCLE

The material of the Earth's crust is constantly changing, usually through plate-tectonic activity.

Rocks melt and are solidified as igneous rocks. These may break down when exposed and become sedimentary rocks or may be changed into metamorphic rocks. These then may break down again. This is known as the *rock cycle*.

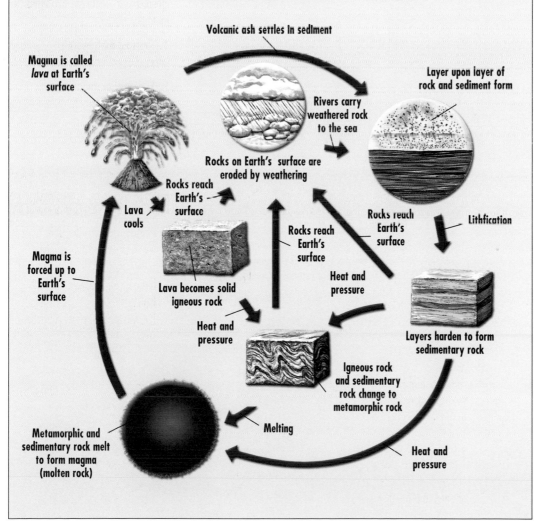

Volcanic ash settles in sediment

Magma is called *lava* at Earth's surface

Rivers carry weathered rock to the sea

Layer upon layer of rock and sediment form

Rocks on Earth's surface are eroded by weathering

Rocks reach Earth's surface

Lava cools

Rocks reach Earth's surface

Lithfication

Magma is forced up to Earth's surface

Lava becomes solid igneous rock

Rocks reach Earth's surface

Heat and pressure

Heat and pressure

Layers harden to form sedimentary rock

Igneous rock and sedimentary rock change to metamorphic rock

Metamorphic and sedimentary rock melt to form magma (molten rock)

Melting

Heat and pressure

EXAMPLES OF METAMORPHIC ROCK

- **Marble** (thermal) is formed as limestone is cooked by igneous activity.

- **Slate** (regional) is formed as mountain-building activities push on sedimentary rocks, such as shale. It splits easily along lines of weakness.

- **Schist** (regional) is formed by more intense mountain-building activities. New minerals are formed along twisted bands.

- **Gneiss** (regional) is formed in the extreme depths of mountains and has big, obvious crystals.

Gneiss

FOSSILS

We know that animals and plants existed long ago on the Earth. They have left their remains behind as fossils. These may be parts of the original organisms or traces, such as footprints, that they left behind. Fossils give unique insight into what kinds of life lived millions of years ago. How they grew, if and how they cared for their young, and what they are are many of the things we have discovered from studying fossils.

HOW FOSSILS FORM

Fossils form in different ways and can be classed on how much of the original creature is left.

1. Organisms preserved in their entirety. These are very rare and include things like insects entombed in amber.

2. The hard parts of living things preserved unaltered, such as sharks' teeth in Tertiary sediments.

3. Only some of the original substance of the living thing left. Leaves can break down leaving a thin film of the original carbon in the shape of the leaf. This produces coal.

4. Petrified living things. The original organic substance is replaced molecule by molecule to produce a fossil with the original structure but made entirely of mineral. Petrified wood is created by this process.

5. Mould. This is a hole left in the rock when all the original organic material has decayed away. A special kind of mould forms from the hollow between the shells of a bivalve seashell.

6. Cast. When a mould (see E) is filled by minerals deposited by ground water, the result is a lump in the shape of the original body, but does not have the internal structure. A cast can form in the space between the valves of seashells, showing us the shape of the interior of the shells.

7. Trace fossils. Sometimes nothing of the original organism is left — just its burrows or the marks that it made, showing us how it lived but not what it looked like. Dinosaur footprints are important trace fossils.

Petrified wood

THE USES OF FOSSILS

Apart from showing us the history of life on Earth, fossils can be used for a number of purposes.

Index fossils Some animals or plants only existed for a short period of time. When the fossils of those animals are found in rock, the rock must have formed during that time. By observing the presence of fossils with overlapping time periods, the date of that rock can be more precise.

Facies fossil Some animals or plants can only live under specific environmental conditions. When the fossils of these creatures are found, the rocks in which they are entombed must have formed under these conditions. Facies fossils are important to oil geologists who are looking for rocks that formed under the right conditions to produce oil.

BEFORE FOSSILIZATION

Many things can happen to an organism before it is fossilized.

• It can be eaten, or partially eaten, by other animals.

• It may rot away.

• It may break down under the influence of the weather.

This is why it is very unlikely for any individual organism to be preserved as a fossil. Activity before fossilization is known as *taphonomy*.

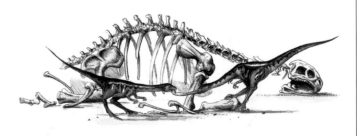

DURING FOSSILIZATION

- For an organism to become a fossil it must be buried rapidly in sediment. This will ensure that none of the taphonomic effects will take place.
- This is why most of the fossils found are of animals that live in the water, where sediment is accumulating, and why fossils of land-living animals are very rare.
- The remains are then affected in various ways, producing the different fossil types.
- The process that takes place as the sediment becomes sedimentary rock, is known as *diagenesis*.

FOSSIL ASSEMBLAGES

Fossils are not usually found individually. Many are found together as groups called *assemblages*.

Life assemblage This occurs when the fossils reflect how the animals and plants lived. In a life assemblage, the bivalve molluscs are still joined together and attached animals like sea lilies are in their growth positions. It is as if the whole community had just dropped dead on the spot. This is very valuable in determining how the animals lived.

Death assemblage This occurs when the dead animals and plants are carried by currents and end up all jumbled together. We can identify a death assemblage by the fact that bivalve shells are broken apart and may be aligned in the direction of the current, delicate skeletons are disarticulated and scattered, and fossils from nearby environments are mixed up with them.

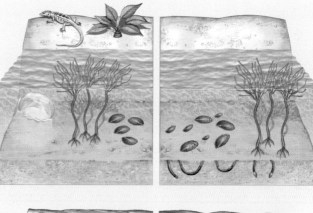

Death assemblage (left) and life assemblage (right).

AFTER FOSSILIZATION

Once a fossil is formed, it lies deep beneath the surface of the Earth, maybe several miles down.

It must be brought to the surface to be found. This usually happens if the sedimentary rocks that contain it are caught up in mountain-building processes through the actions of plate tectonics. The rocks may be twisted and crushed up so much that they end up as mountains well above sea level. The wind and the rain then break them down, forming new material for clastic sedimentary rocks.

The fossil-bearing beds may then be exposed to our view.

• See pages 8–9 PLATE TECHTONICS

Finding dinosaur fossils.

PRECAMBRIAN (2,500–543 MYA) TIMELINE

Proterozoic	Neoproterozoic	
	Mesoproterozoic	
	Paleoproterozoic	
Archaean		
Hadean		

(labelled: Precambrain)

During much of Precambrian, life was developing from mere molecules that had the ability to reproduce, such as viruses, through the formation of single cells, such as bacteria, to creatures that were made up of many cells. Some of these creatures were the precursors of today's life forms.

EVIDENCE OF LIFE TIMELINE

3.5 million years
Signs of where microbes may have eaten into newly erupted basalt flows on the sea bed.

600 million years
The earliest known multicelled organisms, like sea anemones come from the Mackenzie Mountains in Canada.

0.8 billion years
Evidence of life can be found in the Bitter Springs Chert in Australia.

2 billion years
Gunflint chert microfossils show evidence of life in Canada.

3.465 billion years
Possible lifeforms in microfossils in the Apex Chert in Australia.

3.5 billion years
Microfossils in Swaziland show signs of life. (The chert in which most of these are found is a glassy sedimentary rock made of silica)

VENDIAN PERIOD

The very end of the Neoproterozoic is known as the *Vendian*. Fossils of multi-celled animals are known from this period, but none with a hard shell.

Many scientists like to include the Vendian in the Paleozoic era rather than the Precambrian.

PRECAMBRIAN WORLD

The Precambrian lasts over 85 percent of the Earth's history.

During the Precambrian, the continents were very small, with the Earth almost completely covered by water.

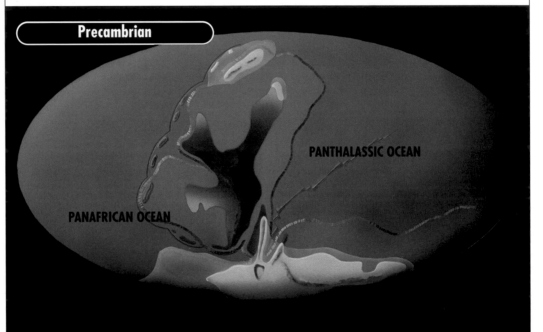

Precambrian

PANTHALASSIC OCEAN

PANAFRICAN OCEAN

STROMATOLITES

The earliest good fossils discovered are of stromatolites.

These occur when microscopic filaments of algae or bacteria attract particles of sediment and form a mat. Other mats build up on this to form a dome-like structure. The oldest stromatolites are 3.5 billion years old.

Today, they are found in the Red Sea and around Australia in sheltered salty bays where there are no other living things to disturb their growth.

A fossilized stromatolite

Modern stromatolites in Australia.

SNOWBALL EARTH

It is possible that between 750 and 580 million years ago, the Earth was entirely frozen. As this was just before many-celled animals appeared, it is possible that the return to more temperate climates, after such a drastic event, spurred the burst in evolution.

Evidence

- Glaciated rocks in Australia and other continents from that time formed at sea level near the equator.

- Limestones formed at that time show evidence that they would have formed in very cold water.

- Lack of oxygen in the atmosphere is shown by the minerals formed at that time. This would come about if cold conditions killed off nearly all life.

What the Earth may have looked like 750-580 million years ago.

ANIMALS OF THE VENDIAN

The first living things were molecules that could reproduce themselves from the chemicals around them. Eventually, they became single-celled organisms, first with simple prokaryotic cells, and then with more complex eukaryotic cells. The latter eventually developed into multi-celled types. The cells formed tissues that built up into individual organs. Amongst the earliest multi-celled organisms were strange soft-bodied organisms from the Vendian period in Australia and of England. These include Spriggina, which resembled a segmented worm, and Charnodiscus, a feather-like animal found on the seafloor.

Spriggina

Charnodiscus

EARLY PALEOZOIC TIMELINE

543–417 MYA

Early Paleozoic Era	Silurian	Pridoli
		Ludlow
		Wenlock
		Llandovery
	Ordovician	Bala
		Dyfed
		Canadian
	Cambrian	Merioneth
		St David's
		Caerfai

PALAEOZOIC ERA

The Palaeozoic era is made up of six periods.
The first three periods make up the early Palaeozoic era. the other three are the Devonian, Carboniferous, and Permian.

Permian 290–248 MYA

Carboniferous 354–290 MYA

Devonian 417–354 MYA

early Palaeozoic 543–417 MYA

LAND ANIMALS

Although we believe there were no land animals in the early Paleozoic, some strange trace fossils from Canada, from the Cambrian period have been found.
They were made by a soft-bodied animal. The animal moved along the damp sand of the Cambrian shoreline. The animal had flaps on either side of its body and dug those into the sand to pull itself forward, creating tracks that look like motorcycle tracks.

EARLY PALEOZOIC ERA

During the early Paleozoic era, many different kinds of hard-shelled animals have evolved in the sea. By the end of the early Paleozoic, however, some life was beginning to venture out of the water and live on dry land.

SILURIAN PERIOD

Meaning: *From Silures* – an old Welsh tribe.
Continents were continuing to move together. The edges of the continents were flooded, giving large areas of shallow sea over continental shelves. Many reefs and shallow-water organisms existed at that time. The first land-living plants appeared.

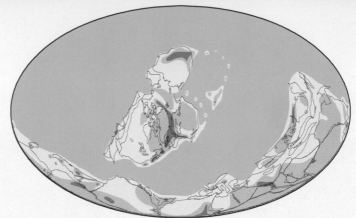

ORDOVICIAN PERIOD

Meaning: *From Ordovices* – an old Welsh tribe.
In the Ordovician period, the northern landmasses were beginning to move toward one another. An ice age took place at the boundary with the Silurian, 450 to 440 million years ago.

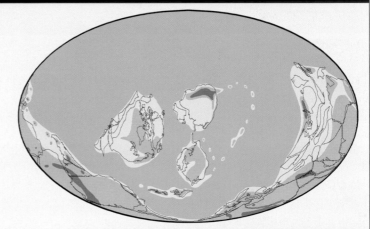

CAMBRIAN PERIOD

Meaning: *From Cambria* – an old name for Wales, where the original work was done on the lower Paleozoic rocks.
In the early Paleozoic, all of the southern continents, South America, Africa, India, Australia and Antarctica, were part of a single landmass. The northern continents, North America, Europe, and Asia, were individual landmasses scattered over the ocean.

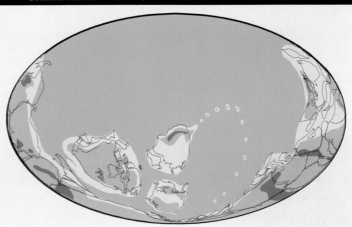

THE BURGESS SHALE

The most spectacular set of Cambrian fossils lies in the Burgess Shale in Canada. These consist of all kinds of animals, most of which do not fit into any established classification.

Burgess shale animals
Marella — like a trilobite with long horns on its head.
Nectocaris — like a shrimp's body with an eel's tail.
Opabinia — like a worm with a trunk and many pairs of paddles.
Wiwaxia — like a slug covered in chain mail.
Hallucigenia — a worm-like body with tentacles along one side and stilts along the other.
Anomalocaris — a big swimming predator that probably hunted all these.

• See page 55 for more information on CHARLES DOOLITTLE WALCOTT who discovered the Burgess Shale.

The Burgess Shale in Canada today.

CALYMENE

Time: Silurian
Size: About 1 $\frac{3}{16}$ in.
Diet: Organic particles from sea bed
Habitat: Shallow seas
Information: *Calymene* was a typical trilobite — one of the most abundant of the sea-living arthropods in the early Paleozoic.

Pygidium — tail shield made from fused segments

Thorax — central part of body made up of segments

Cephalon — head shield

DIPLOGRAPTUS

Time: Silurian
Size: 2 in., each branch
Diet: Suspended organic particles
Habitat: Open water
Information: *Diplograptus* was a common graptolite — a floating colonial organism. It consisted of two rows of living creatures back to back, and several hanging suspended from a gas float.

Other graptolites include *Monograptus*, with a single row of individuals, and *Didymograptus*, with two rows arranged in a wishbone shape. These are all valuable index fossils for the early Paleozoic.

• See pages 12–13 for more information on INDEX FOSSILS.

ANIMAL PROFILES

Isotelus
Period: Silurian
Diet: Buried organic matter
Habitat: In sandy sea bottoms
Information: Spade-shaped trilobite, smooth surface, adapted for burrowing.

Cryptolithus
Period: Ordovician
Diet: Floating organic matter
Habitat: Open water
Information: Free-swimming trilobite, huge cephalon with long spines at the rear, small thorax and pygidium.

Eodiscus
Period: Cambrian
Diet: Floating organic matter
Habitat: Open water
Information: Tiny early trilobite, free swimming, only two segments in the thorax, cephalon the same size as pygidium.

Olenellus
Period: Cambrian
Diet: Organic detritus
Habitat: Shallow sea bed
Information: An early trilobite, tiny pygidium, spines on the segments.

DEVONIAN TIMELINE

417–354 MYA

Devonian period	Famennian Frasnian	D3
	Givetian Eifelian	D2
	Emsian Pragian Lochkovian	D1

During this period, animals began to leave the water and live on land. In the previous Silurian period, land plants first appeared. The first land-living animals were insects, living in this vegetation. Then came the vertebrates in transitional forms between fish and amphibians. They would have been attracted by the new food supplies on land, or may have taken refuge from the ferocious fish and sea scorpions that lived in the water.

PLANTS

The earliest land plants were nothing but a stem that supported a reproductive body. By the end of the Devonian, there were forests of horsetails and ferns.

THE AGE OF FISH

Although fish had already evolved, they did not become important until the Devonian, also known as the *Age of Fish*.

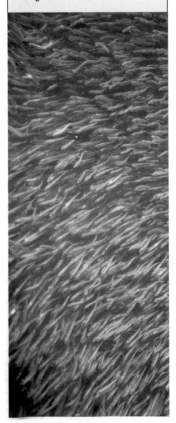

THE WORLD IN THE DEVONIAN PERIOD

The Devonian period is named after the county of Devon in the United Kingdom, where many rocks of this period have been found.

During this time, the continents were beginning to move together. The land that will become Europe and North America collided, forming a single continent, called *Old Red Sandstone*, with an enormous mountain range up between the two. The remains of this mountain range are found in the Scottish and Norwegian Highlands and part of the Appalachians in North America.

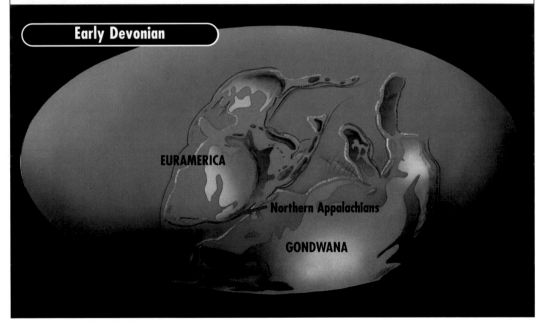

Early Devonian

EURAMERICA

Northern Appalachians

GONDWANA

CHANGING ATMOSPHERE

The atmosphere during the early part of Earth's history was a toxic mix of poisonous gases that no animal could breathe. By the Devonian it had changed, with oxygen being added to the atmosphere by plant life in the water and on land. This made it possible for the land to be habitated.

Atmosphere at the Earth's beginning

Other 3%
N 12%
H_2 10%
CO_2 75%

Precambrian atmosphere

CO_2 10%
Other 15%
N 75%

Devonian atmosphere

O_2 25%
N 75%

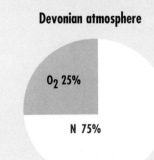

OLD RED SANDSTONE

This type of rock is typical of the Devonian period. Formed from river gravels and desert sandstones, it turned red through oxidation of iron in it by exposure to air.

• See pages 10–11 for more information on *TYPES OF ROCK*.

• See pages 10–11 for more information on *TYPES OF ROCK*.

CEPHALASPIS

Meaning: Head spike
Time: Late Silurian – Early Devonian
Size: 50 cm (19 ft 5 in).
Diet: Organic detritus.
Habitat: Shallow water.
Information: This early fish had no jaws, just a sucker to allow it to scoop up food from the sea bed.

EUSTHENOPTERON

Meaning: *Properly strong fin*
Time: Late Devonian
Size: 3 ft. 3 in.
Diet: Other fish
Habitat: Shorelines
Information: A fish that shows adaptations to life on land. Its fins were in pairs and had bones and muscles, allowing it to move over dry surfaces. A lung enabled it to breathe air.

ICHTHYOSTEGA

Meaning: *Fish-roof*
Time: Late Devonian
Size: 3 ft. 3 in.
Diet: Fish and insects
Habitat: Shorelines
Information: One of the earliest of amphibians. *Ichthyostega* still had a fish's skull and tail. Its hind limbs had eight toes—the standard five-toed pattern had not yet evolved.

ANIMAL PROFILES

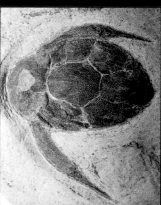

Dunkleosteus
Period: Late Devonian
Diet: Other fish
Habitat: Open ocean
Information: A giant form of the armored fish—one of the biggest of the time.

Cladoselache
Period: Late Devonian
Diet: Other fish
Habitat: Open ocean
Information: An early shark, very similar looking to modern forms—the shape of sharks has not changed much over the years.

Bothriolepis
Period: Early Devonian
Diet: Organic detritus
Habitat: Lakes
Information: A group of armored fish, common in the Devonian period. It had armored jointed and front fins.

Climatius
Period: Early Devonian
Diet: Other fish
Habitat: River mouths
Information: One of the so-called *spiny sharks*, with heavy scales and a double row of fins along its belly.

CARBONIFEROUS TIMELINE
354–290 MYA

Carboniferous Period		
Pennsylvanian	Gzelian
	Kasimovian
	Moscovian
	Bashkirian
Mississippian	Serpukhovian
	Visean
	Tournaisian

By the Carboniferous period, life on the land had become fully established. Coal forests are inhabited by gigantic insects and other arthropods. The first reptiles begin to emerge during this time. The period came to an end with an ice age that affected most of the southern hemisphere.

ONE PERIOD OR TWO?

In Europe, the Carboniferous is regarded as a single period. In America, it is split in two.

Pennsylvanian – 323–290 MYA
Equivalent to the late Carboniferous or the upper Carboniferous.

Mississippian – 354–323 MYA
Equivalent to the early Carboniferous or the lower Carboniferous.

Upper and *lower* are terms used when talking about the rock sequences or the fossils formed. *Early* and *late* are terms used when talking about the events of the time, such as the evolution of reptiles.

THE WORLD IN THE CARBONIFEROUS PERIOD

The period is named after the element *carbon*, which was abundant at this time.
During the Carboniferous, mountain ranges were being quickly eroded and the debris spread out into broad river deltas. The deltas were covered in thick forests that eventually formed the coal seams of the period.

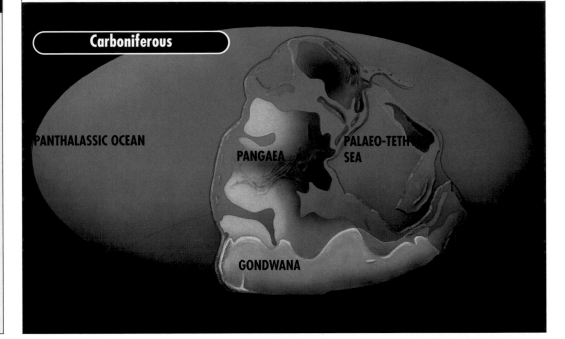

Carboniferous

PANTHALASSIC OCEAN

PANGAEA

PALAEO-TETHYS SEA

GONDWANA

FORMATION OF COAL

1. The plant layers soaked up water and were pressed together, forming a brown, spongy material, called *peat*.

3. More heat and pressure, at greater depths, turned the lignite into a soft, black coal, called *bituminous coal*.

2. More sediment layers formed on top of the peat, burying it deeper and deeper. The greater pressure and heat turned the peat into a brown coal, called *lignite*.

4. This finally turned into a harder, shiny black coal, called *anthracite*.

COAL FOREST PLANTS

Lepidodendron – a club moss that grew up to 100 ft. high. It consisted of a straight trunk that branched dichotomously (into two equal branches, then into two again) with long strap-shaped leaves. Trunk covered in diamond-shaped leaf scars.

Sigillaria – a club moss similar to *Lepidodendron* but with leaf scars arranged in parallel rows.

Calamites – horsetails as big as 7 feet tall. Grew as reed beds in shallow water.

Cordaites – a primitive relative of the conifers that grew on slightly drier ground. Various ferns formed undergrowth and creeping up the trunks.

EOGYRINUS

Meaning: *Early twister*
Time: Late Carboniferous
Size: 16 ft. 4 in.
Diet: Fish and other amphibians
Habitat: Coal swamps

Information: One of the big amphibians of the period, it cruised the shallow waters of the coal swamp like an alligator, looking for other animals to eat. *Eogyrinus* could spend some time on land, but it needed to return to the water to breed.

MEGANEURA

Meaning: *Big nerves*
Time: Late Carboniferous
Size: 4 ft. 9 in. wingspan.
Diet: Unknown
Information: Like a dragonfly, but the size of a bird, *Meganeura* was typical of the very large arthropods that existed in the coal forests. Other anthropods included centipedes as big as pythons.

WESTLOTHIANA

Meaning: *From the county of Westlothian in Scotland*
Time: Early Carboniferous
Size: 7 $\frac{7}{8}$ in.
Diet: Small insects

Information: *Westlothiana* is either the earliest reptile known, or it is something between the amphibians and the reptiles. It was certainly the precursor of the land-living animals to come.

ANIMAL PROFILES

Hylonomus
Period: Late Carboniferous
Diet: Insects
Habitat: In the trunks of coal forest trees
Information: An early reptile, like a modern lizard.

Diplovertebron
Period: Late Carboniferous
Diet: Insects and other amphibians
Habitat: Coal swamps
Information: A big amphibian.

Ophiderpeton
Period: Late Carboniferous
Diet: Small invertebrates
Habitat: Moist leaf litter
Information: An amphibian without legs and lived like an earthworm in the ground cover.

Arthroplura
Period: Late Carboniferous
Diet: Rotting vegetable matter
Habitat: Coal swamps
Information: A gigantic millipede, 5 ft. 9 in. long.

Crassigyrinus
Period: Early Carboniferous
Diet: Fish and other amphibians
Habitat: Coal swamps
Information: Amphibian with tiny limbs, a big head and a tapering body.

21

	Zechstein	Changxingian
		Longtanian
Permian Period		Capitanian
		Wordian
		Ufimian
	Rotliegendes	Kungurian
		Artinskian
		Sakmarian
		Asselian

DESERT FEATURES

Desert features seen in Permian rocks:
- Dune bedding
- Red sandstones showing dry oxidation environments
- Beds of coarse pebbles that have been shaped by the wind

PERMIAN PERIOD

At the beginning of the Permian period, the southern hemisphere was still in the grip of the ice age that started at the end of the Carboniferous period. Once the ice age ended, the Earth entered a desert period, forming the *New Red Sandstone* layer. The end of the Permian period shows a large amount of volcanic activity, mostly in what will become Siberia.

THE WORLD IN THE PERMIAN PERIOD

This period is named after the Perm region in Russia, where the rocks dating from this time are well exposed. In the Permian, nearly all the continents had accumulated into a single landmass. The mountains during the Devonian and Carboniferous periods were eroded into hills, and there was less erosion forming river deltas. The coal forests dried up and were replaced by deserts.

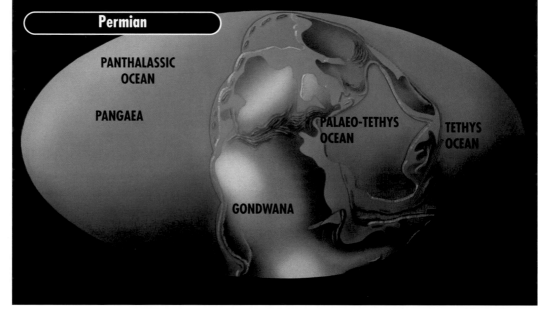

Permian

PANTHALASSIC OCEAN

PANGAEA

PALAEO-TETHYS OCEAN

TETHYS OCEAN

GONDWANA

REEFS

The kinds of sea animals in earlier began to die out during the Permian period. In the region of Texas, there were thick reefs. Modern reefs are made of corals. Permian reefs were made of:

- Sponges
- Algae
- Bivalves
- Crinoids (sea lilies)
- Brachiopods (animal with two shells but unrelated to bivalves)

The Permian reefs of Texas contain the state's oil reserves.

MESOSAURUS

Meaning: *Middle lizard*
Time: Early Permian
Size: 3 ft. 3 in.
Diet: Small swimming animals
Information: The age of reptiles had arrived, with swimming, flying, and land-living types. Fossils of *Mesosaurus*, a freshwater swimmer, have been found in South Africa and Brazil, showing that this area was all one continent at that time.

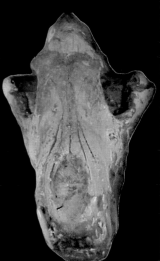

Moschops
Period: Late Permian
Diet: Plants
Habitat: Deserts
Information: A big plant-eating, mammal-like reptile.

Eryops
Period: Late Permian
Diet: Fish and other amphibians
Habitat: Desert streams
Information: One of the big amphibians that still existed at this time.

Lycaenops
Period: Late Permian
Diet: Other reptiles
Habitat: Deserts
Information: A mammal-like reptile that looked like a mammal.

Seymouria
Period: Early Permian
Diet: Insects and small vertebrates
Habitat: Deserts
Information: Had features that were transitional between amphibians and reptiles.

PAREIASAURUS

Meaning: *Side-by-side lizard*
Time: Middle Permian
Size: 8 ft. 2 in.
Diet: Plants
Information: Plant-eating vertebrates appeared at this time. Big-bodied types like *Pareiasaurus* fed on the ferns and conifers found at desert ouses.

DIMETRODON

Meaning: *Two sizes of tooth*
Time: Early Permian
Size: 9 ft. 8 in.
Diet: Other reptiles
Information: An important group of reptiles were the mammal like reptiles that eventually gave rise to the mammals. *Dimetrodon* was an early example. It had a sail on its back to help regulate its temperature in the desert heat.

Triassic Period	Rhaetian	
	Norian	Tr₃
	Carnian	
	Ladinian	Tr₂
	Anisian	
	Spathian	
	Nammalian	Scythian, Tr1
	Griesbachian	

MESOZOIC ERA

The Triassic period is the first of the three periods that make up the Mesozoic era.

Cretaceous 144–65 MYA

Jurassic 206–144 MYA

Triassic 248–206 MYA

GLOSSOPTERIS

A new kind of plant—*Glossopteris* (a kind of fern that reproduced by seed)—became very common. Its fossils are found throughout the southern continents.

TRIASSIC PERIOD

After the Permian period ends, Earth began to change dramatically. The boundary between the Permian and the Triassic periods coincided with the greatest mass-extinction in Earth's history, 95 percent of all species were wiped out. It is not known whether the volcanic activity in what will become Siberia had anything to do with it, but following the event, whole new groups of animals spread over the land and sea.

THE WORLD IN THE TRIASSIC PERIOD

All the continents had now come together to form one great supercontinent, called **Pangaea**.

All of the oceans were combined into one ocean, called *Panthalassa*. The New Red Sandstone conditions continued, with arid deserts in the hinterland of the continent. Land life was only possible around the coast line.

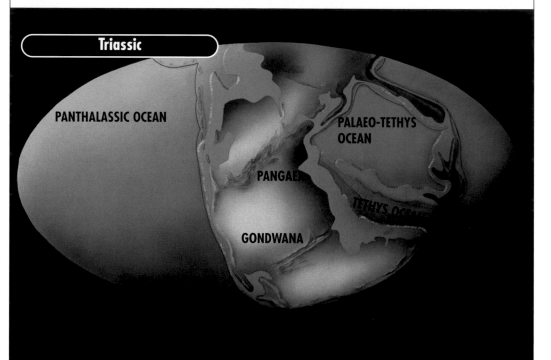

Triassic

PANTHALASSIC OCEAN

PALAEO-TETHYS OCEAN

PANGAEA

TETHYS OCEAN

GONDWANA

MEANING OF THE NAME

Trias — *three*. Refers to the three sequences of rock in Germany where the period was first identified. These are:
Keuper — desert sandstones and marls.
Muschelkalk — *mussel chalk*. Limestone marking a marine phase.
Bunter — *desert sandstones*.
Classification still used, even though in most of Europe, the Muschelkalk is absent.

Muschelkalk

NEW PLANT LIFE

There were many differences between the plants of the Permian and Triassic periods.

Trees
Permian – giant club mosses and cordaites, just like the Carboniferous coal forests.

Triassic – primitive conifers like monkey puzzle trees.

Medium-sized plants
Permian – giant horsetails, tree ferns.

Triassic – cycad-like plants, tree ferns.

Small plants
Permian – seed ferns and horsetails.

Triassic – conventional ferns and horsetails.

REASONS FOR THE MASS EXTINCTION

There are several theories for the mass extinction.

1. The change to the atmosphere caused by the eruptions in Siberia.
2. Climate fluctuation caused by the joining of all the continents.
3. Chemical evidence has been found in Australia and Antarctica of a meteorite impact, but it is not strong evidence.
4. Change in the salt content of the ocean.

TRIASSIC CLIMATES

Because all the land was in a single supercontinent, the climates were extreme. They could be divided into a number of belts.
1. Year round dry climate.
2. Seasonal rainfall near the coasts.
3. High latitude regions with cool rains.
The interior of Pangaea was extremely hot during the Triassic, with little rain falling. Warm temperatures extended down to the Earth's poles. Scientists think that this was one of the hottest periods of the planet's history, with gobal warming occurring toward the end of the Triassic.

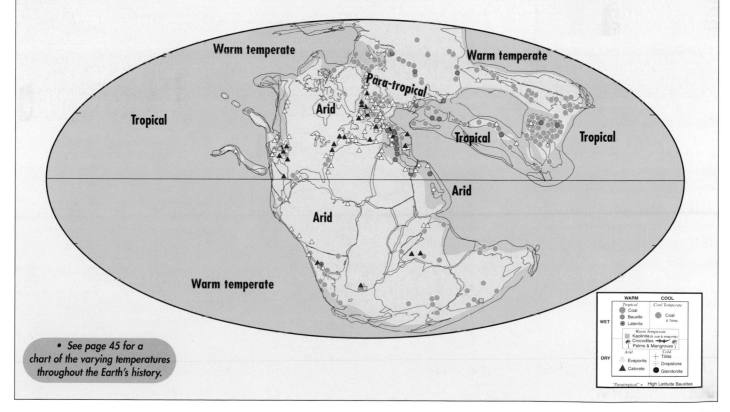

• *See page 45 for a chart of the varying temperatures throughout the Earth's history.*

TRIASSIC LIFE

There was a significant change of life in the Triassic period. The varied sea creatures of the Paleozoic era were gone, replaced by totally new types of water-living animals. The changed plant life on land provided food for the new animal life. Land animals continued to develop and expand; some developed the ability to fly or swim. It is during the Triassic period that the first mammals and dinosaurs appear.

HARD-SHELLED EGG: THE KEY TO LAND-LIVING

At the begining of the Age of Reptiles, there were still plenty of big amphibians on Earth.

- Reptiles have hard-shelled eggs. Amphibians lay soft eggs that must remain in water.

- Reptiles hatch fully formed from the egg. Amphibians go through a larval "tadpole" stage, usually in the water.

- Reptiles have a tough waterproof skin that can stand up to dry conditions. Amphibians have a soft skin covered in mucus that must be kept moist.

CHANGING PLANTS, CHANGING ANIMALS

The evolving plant life encouraged an evolving animal life as well. The plant-eating mammal-like reptiles declined as the seed-ferns died out. A new line of plant-eating mammal-like reptile evolved as the conventional ferns took over. Mammals and dinosaurs evolved, and the conifers established themselves at the end of the period.

Dinosaurs evolved to eat the conifers.

New reptiles, called rhynchosaurs evolved to eat the conventional ferns.

Mammal-like reptiles ate seed-ferns.

FOOTPRINTS

Evidence of reptile existence comes from the many footprints found in Triassic sandstones.

Famous localities include, Dinosaur State Park in Connecticut, Moab, Utah, and Dumfriesshire, Scotland.

• See pages 12–13 for more information on FOSSILS.

WHAT MAKES A DINOSAUR?

There are several features that define a dinosaur and make it different from all other reptiles.

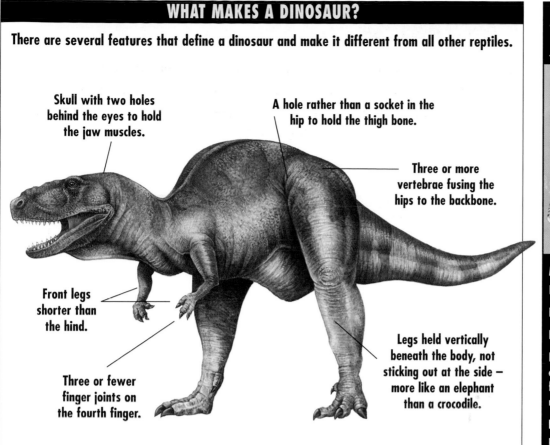

Skull with two holes behind the eyes to hold the jaw muscles.

A hole rather than a socket in the hip to hold the thigh bone.

Three or more vertebrae fusing the hips to the backbone.

Front legs shorter than the hind.

Three or fewer finger joints on the fourth finger.

Legs held vertically beneath the body, not sticking out at the side — more like an elephant than a crocodile.

EORAPTOR

Meaning: *Early hunter*
Time: Late Triassic
Size: ft. 3 in.
Diet: Small animals
Information: The earliest dinosaur known. Having all the features of an early meat-eating dinosaur — a bipedal stance with the head out to the front, balanced by a heavy tail, small clawed hands, and long jaws with sharp teeth.

EUDIMORPHODON

Meaning: *True two shapes of teeth*
Time: Late Triassic
Size: 3 ft. 3 in. wingspan
Diet: Fish
Information: One of the earliest *pterosaurs* — a group of flying reptiles, related to dinosaurs, that were the lords of the skies in the Mesozoic era. *Eudimorphodon's* wings were formed by wing membranes supported by a long finger.

THECODONTOSAURUS

Meaning: *Socket-toothed lizard*
Time: Late Triassic
Size: 3 ft. 3 in.
Diet: Plants
Information: One of the first of the plant-eating dinosaurs. *Thecodontosaurus* had a larger body than a meat-eater, to hold a more complex digestive system, and a small head and a long neck to reach its food.

JURASSIC PERIOD

JURASSIC TIMELINE

206–144 MYA

	Malm	Tithonian
Jurassic Period		Kimmeridgian
		Oxfordian
	Dogger	Callovian
		Bathonian
		Bajocian
		Aalenian
	Lias	Toarcian
		Pliensbachian
		Sinemurian
		Hettangian

Although the dinosaurs appeared in the previous period, the Triassic, it was during the Jurassic period that they took over and became the most dominant creatures on Earth at that time. There were fewer deserts then, because the supercontinent of Pangaea was splitting up and spreading arms of the ocean and shallow seas across the landmass.

THE WORLD IN THE JURASSIC PERIOD

The beginning the Jurassic period was still a time of deserts. However, as the age progressed, rift valleys appeared across Pangaea, and the supercontinent began to break up.

The most famous rift valley was the zig-zag rift that began to split the Americas from Europe and Africa. This would eventually form the Atlantic Ocean.

As North America began to move westward, the Rocky Mountains began to build up before it.

MASS EXTINCTIONS

There were three mass-extinction events that took place at this time.

1. At the boundary between the Triassic and Jurassic. This killed the last of the mammal-like reptiles.

2. During the Pleinsbachian stage of the lower Jurassic. This affected much of the dinosaur life.

3. At the very end of the Jurassic period. This had a greater effect on sea animals than land animals.

None of these were particularly large.

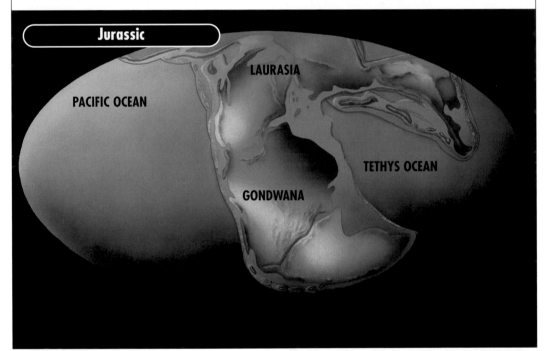

Jurassic

PACIFIC OCEAN

LAURASIA

GONDWANA

TETHYS OCEAN

MEANING OF THE NAME

The Jurassic is named after the Jura Mountains, where Alexander von Humboldt first studied limestones in 1795. He named this period *Jurassic* in 1799.

TYPICAL JURASSIC ROCKS

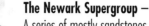

Oolitic limestone — Chemical sedimentary rock made up of fine pellets of calcite. Good as a building material.

Lias — A series of interbedded limestone and deep water shale from the earliest part of the period. It was laid down as deep water muds, and the limestone separated out as it solidified.

• See pages 10–11 for more information on different TYPES OF ROCK.

TWO JURASSIC ROCK SEQUENCES

The Newark Supergroup — A series of mostly sandstones, laid down in rift valleys along the east coast of North America, showing where Pangaea began to break apart.

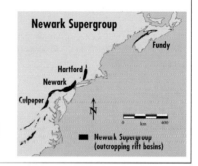

Newark Supergroup

Fundy

Hartford
Newark

Culpeper

N

0   km   400

■ Newark Supergroup
(outcropping rift basins)

The Morrison Formation — A sequence of river sandstones, shales, conglomerates, and evaporates laid down on an arid plain. It was crossed by rivers in the late Jurassic period of the American midwest.

ECONOMIC IMPORTANCE

The rocks that formed in the Jurassic period are extremely important in today's world as building materials and fuel.

• The oilfields of the North Sea are Jurassic rocks.
• Much of London is built from late Jurassic Portland limestone.

Rhomaleosaurus

Period: Early Jurassic

Diet: Fish

Habitat: Shallow seas

Information: A plesiosaur with a big head—almost an intermediate form between plesiosaurs (long-necked) and pliosaurs (short-necked).

Ichthyosaurus

Period: Early Jurassic

Diet: Fish

Habitat: Open ocean

Info: A medium-sized ichthyosaur that resembled a modern-day shark. It had a slim, pointed snout and foreflippers twice as large as its hind flippers.

INDEX FOSSILS

The different marine beds of the Jurassic are dated using species of ammonites, relatives of squids and cuttlefish. that left fossils of coiled shells.

Each species existed only for a few million years, so the rocks where they were found can be closely dated. Each species was quite widespread throughout the ocean, so their fossils are common in different parts of the world.

JURASSIC LIFE

Fossils of sea-living animals are more abundant than those of land-living ones, because the majority of fossils are found in marine deposits. This does not mean that life was more abundant in the water than on land during the Jurassic period, just that it was easier for marine animal remains to become fossilized. The growing seas gave rise to broad continental shelves where sediment built up and trapped the fossils of the sea life of the time.

THE LIFE ON A CONTINENTAL SHELF

The animal life near the shore was different from that in the open water, which again was different from that of the deep sea bed. Many species have been preserved as fossils in marine limestone and shale.

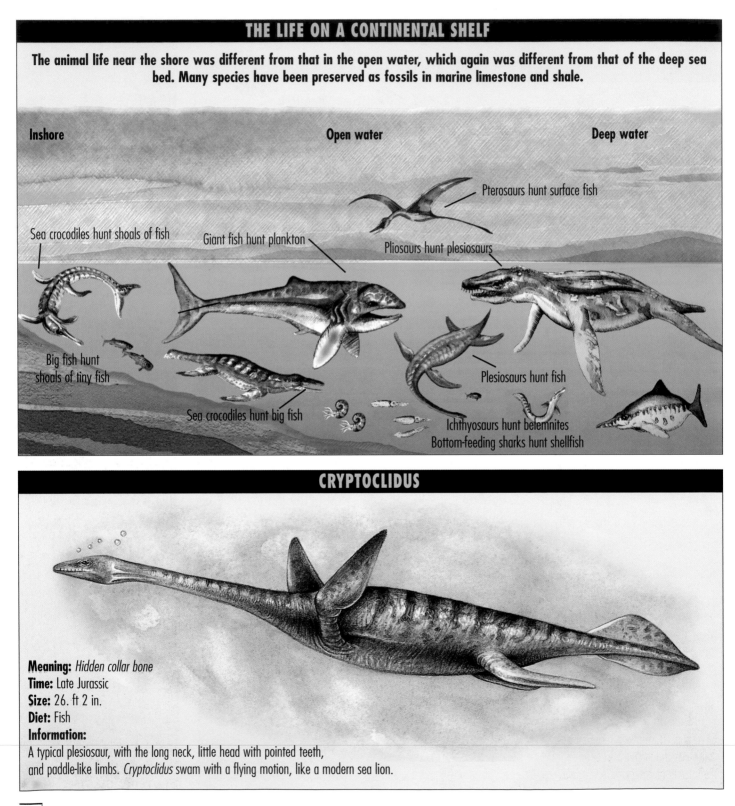

Inshore

Open water

Deep water

Pterosaurs hunt surface fish

Sea crocodiles hunt shoals of fish

Giant fish hunt plankton

Pliosaurs hunt plesiosaurs

Big fish hunt shoals of tiny fish

Plesiosaurs hunt fish

Sea crocodiles hunt big fish

Ichthyosaurs hunt belemnites
Bottom-feeding sharks hunt shellfish

CRYPTOCLIDUS

Meaning: *Hidden collar bone*
Time: Late Jurassic
Size: 26. ft 2 in.
Diet: Fish
Information:
A typical plesiosaur, with the long neck, little head with pointed teeth,
and paddle-like limbs. *Cryptoclidus* swam with a flying motion, like a modern sea lion.

THE FOSSILS OF THE LAGOONS

Along the northern shore of the Tethys Sea—the part of the ocean that separated the north and south parts of Panagea—shallow lagoons formed behind reefs built by sponges and corals.

The bottom of the water was toxic, and it killed and preserved many swimming and flying creatures. These formed minutely-detailed fossils in very fine limestone.

• See pages 12–13 for more information on FOSSILS.

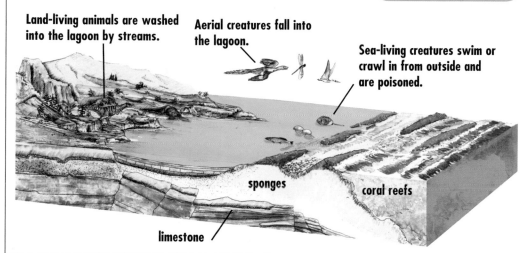

Land-living animals are washed into the lagoon by streams.

Aerial creatures fall into the lagoon.

Sea-living creatures swim or crawl in from outside and are poisoned.

sponges

coral reefs

limestone

LIOPLEURODON

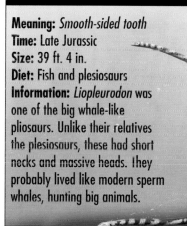

Meaning: *Smooth-sided tooth*
Time: Late Jurassic
Size: 39 ft. 4 in.
Diet: Fish and plesiosaurs
Information: *Liopleurodon* was one of the big whale-like pliosaurs. Unlike their relatives the plesiosaurs, these had short necks and massive heads. They probably lived like modern sperm whales, hunting big animals.

PTERODACTYLUS

Meaning: *Wing finger*
Time: Late Jurassic
Size: 3 ft. 3 in.
Diet: Fish
Information: One of the first of the pterodactyloids, more advanced pterosaurs. These flying reptiles had short tails and longer wrist bones than earlier pterosaurs. *Pterodactylus* can also be distinguished by the angle of the skull and the neck.

ANIMAL PROFILES

Archaeopteryx

Period: Late Jurassic

Diet: Insects

Habitat: Trees

Information: The first bird, but retaining many dinosaur features showing that it was closely related to dinosaurs.

Opthalmosaurus

Period: Late Jurassic

Diet: Fish

Habitat: Shallow seas

Information: A typical ichthyosaur, having developed the well-known fish shape.

Metriorhynchus

Period: Late Jurassic

Diet: Fish

Habitat: Shallow seas

Information: One of the marine crocodiles, with a fish-like tail and paddle limbs.

Leedsihcthys

Period: Late Jurassic

Diet: Plankton and tiny fish

Habitat: Open seas

Information: One of the biggest fish that ever lived, but feeding on small creatures, like the modern whale shark does.

JURASSIC DINOSAURS

The most spectacular animals of Jurassic times were undoubtedly the dinosaurs. They ranged from small fox-sized animals to creatures bigger than modern whales, and they lived on all the continents of the world. Scientists can describe different groups of dinosaurs, each with their own lifestyles and habits.

DINOSAUR TYPES

Saurischians (*Lizard hips*)
These dinosaurs were distinguished by their hips. The three main bones of the hips radiated away from the hole where the leg was attached, as they do in modern lizards.

Ornithischians (*Bird hips*)
In this group of dinosaurs, the pubis bone in the hip is swept back along the ischium bone, making room for a big stomach. They had a bone in the front of the jaw that the saurischians lacked.

Ornithopods (*Bird feet*) The two-footed plant-eaters, although the biggest ones spent most of their time on all fours.

Theropods (*Beast footed*) The meat-eaters, walking on their hind legs, with small arms and the big teeth held out to the front.

Therizinosaurs (*Scythe claws*) These seem to have been plant-eaters, but were closely related to the theropods. Their hips were more like those of the ornithischians.

Marginocephalians Dinosaurs with armored heads. Mostly Cretaceous, they are divided into the boneheads and the horned dinosaurs with the shields around their necks.

Prosauropods (*Before the sauropods*) The earliest plant-eaters, with long necks and small heads.

Thyrophorans Dinosaurs with armor plates. Further divided into the plated stegosaurs (mostly Jurassic) and the armored ankylosaurs (mostly Cretaceous).

Sauropods (*Lizard feet*) The big plant-eating dinosaurs with massive bodies, heavy legs, and very long necks and tails.

A DINOSAUR LANDSCAPE

The most famous dinosaur skeletons were found in the Morrison Formation in western North America. In the Jurassic period, this area was a broad, dry plain between the newly-formed Rocky Mountains and a shallow sea that spread across the center of the continent. The plain was crossed by many rivers, and most dinosaurs lived on the forested river banks.

• See page 29 for more information on the MORRISON FOUNDATION.

ANIMAL PROFILES

Compsognathus
Period: Late Jurassic

Diet: Lizards

Habitat: Island beaches

Information: A theropod, the smallest dinosaur discovered so far.

Ceratosaurus
Period: Late Jurassic

Diet: Other dinosaurs

Habitat: Open plains

Information: A theropod, smaller than *Allosaurus* and armed with a horn on the snout.

Apatosaurus
Period: Late Jurassic

Diet: Plants

Habitat: Open plains

Information: A sauropod very similar to *Diplodocus*, but shorter and more heavily built.

Kentrosaurus
Period: Late Jurassic

Diet: Plants

Habitat: Open plains

Information: A thyreophoran, a stegosaur with very narrow plates and many spines.

Brachiosaurus
Period: Late Jurassic

Diet: Tall trees

Habitat: Open plains

Info: A sauropod that was one of the tallest dinosaurs found.

Megalosaurus
Period: Middle Jurassic

Diet: Other dinosaurs

Habitat: Wooded islands

Information: A theropod, the first dinosaur to be discovered.

STEGOSAURUS

Time: Late Jurassic
Size: 26 ft. 2 in.
Diet: Plants
Information: The plates on the back of *Stegosaurus* were used either for protection or a heat control device. *Stegosaurus* has the smallest brain relative to the size of the animal for any known dinosaur.

DIPLODOCUS

Time: Late Jurassic
Size: 98 ft. 4 in.
Diet: Plants
Information: *Diplodocus* was a typical sauropod. It was balanced at the hips so it could raise itself and reach into trees. *Diplodocus* used its tail as a defensive whip.

CRETACEOUS PERIOD

CRETACEOUS TIMELINE

144–65 MYA

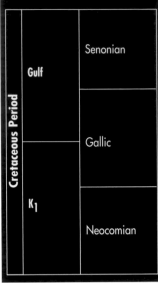

Cretaceous Period	Gulf	Senonian
		Gallic
	K₁	Neocomian

The dinosaurs continued to evolve as the Mesozoic moved forward. During the Cretaceous period, the continents moved away from each other and the dinosaurs diversified. The period was brought to a shuddering end by a sudden event that destroyed the dinosaurs. The age of reptiles was over.

THE WORLD IN THE CRETACEOUS PERIOD

What was left of Pangaea continued to pull apart. Some of the continents were now in the shapes that we would recognize today.

Much of the southern landmass was still present as a supercontinent throughout the Cretaceous. This comprised of what are now South America, Africa, India, Australia, and Antarctica. This supercontinent is called *Gondwana*. Gondwana split up, with only Australia and Antarctica still joined.

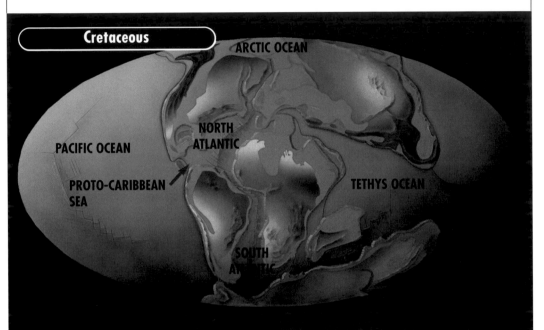

Cretaceous

ARCTIC OCEAN

PACIFIC OCEAN

NORTH ATLANTIC

PROTO-CARIBBEAN SEA

TETHYS OCEAN

SOUTH ATLANTIC

DIVERSE DINOSAURS

There were more dinosaurs around during the Cretaceous than there were previously. This is because all the different isolated continents had different types of dinosaurs evolving on them.

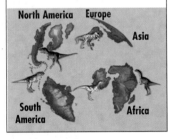

North America Europe
Asia
South America Africa

MEANING OF THE NAME

Creta is the Latin word for *chalk*. Vast deposits of this very fine limestone were laid down on the shallow sea shelves at that time—particularly in southern England, northern France, and Kansas.

• See pages 10–11 TYPES OF ROCK.

TYLOSAURUS

Meaning: *Swollen lizard*
Time: Late Cretaceous
Size: 32 ft. 8 in.
Diet: Ammonites and other sea animals
Information: A typical big mosasaur. Closely related to modern monitor lizards but with paddle-shaped limbs and a flattened tail. *Tylosaurus* and its relatives would have pursued the same prey and had the same lifestyle as the ichthyosaurs of the preceding Jurassic period.

ANIMALS OF AIR AND SEA

The shallow seas that spread everywhere at the end of the period were full of different types of sea animals. The ichthyosaurs were gone, but were replaced by a different group of sea reptiles, the mosasaurs. The pterosaurs continued to rule the skies but birds were present as well.

pterosaurs

mosasaurs

elasmosaurs

pliosaurs

ELASMOSAURUS

Meaning: *Long lizard*
Time: Late Cretaceous
Size: 49 ft. 2 in.
Diet: Fish
Information: *Elasmosaurus* had the longest neck of all the plesiosaurs, comprising 71 vertebrae and taking up more than half the length of the whole animal. It swallowed stones to aid digestion and to adjust its balance while swimming.

KRONOSAURUS

Meaning: *Lizard of Kronos*
Time: Early Cretaceous
Size: 32 ft. 8 in.
Diet: Ammonites and other sea animals
Information: *Kronosaurus* was the biggest of the pliosaurs — certainly the one with the biggest head, 2.7 metres (8 ft 9 in) long. A creature's skull was found in Australia but none of the rest of the body has been unearthed yet.

ARAMBOURGIANIA

Meaning: Named after Camille Arambourg, who first described it in the 1950s
Time: Late Cretaceous
Size: 39 ft. 4 in. wingspan
Diet: Probably fish
Information: Scientists continue finding bigger and bigger pterosaur bones and announcing that this must have been the biggest animal that could possibly fly. The current record holder is *Arambourgiania*.

ANIMAL PROFILES

Alamosaurus

Time: Late Cretaceous

Diet: Trees

Habitat: Woodland

Information: The last sauropod of North America.

Argentinasaurus

Time: Late Cretaceous

Diet: Trees

Habitat: Woodland

Information: A titanosaur. The heaviest dinosaur yet discovered.

Ornithomimus

Time: Late Cretaceous

Diet: Omnivorous

Habitat: Open country

Information: Ostrich-like and very quick.

Protoceratops

Time: Late Cretaceous

Diet: Desert vegetation

Habitat: Desert and scrubland

Information: An early horned-dinosaur.

Sauroposeidon

Time: Early Cretaceous

Diet: Trees

Habitat: Woodland

Information: One of the last and biggest of the brachiosaurs.

Baryonyx

Time: Early Cretaceous

Diet: Fish

Habitat: River banks

Information: A crocodile-snouted fishing theropod.

During the Cretaceous period, the two main groups of dinosaurs, the *saurischians* and the *ornithischians*, continued to be dominate the animal life, but they all developed into different forms on the different continents. Of the saurischians, the plant-eating sauropods were not as important as they had been. The big, meat-eating theropods continued their dominance over other animals. The smaller dinosaurs, however, may have begun the biggest change. Some scientists believed that they evolved as modern birds.

SALTASAURUS

Meaning: *Lizard from Salta*
Time: Late Cretaceous
Size: 39 ft. 4 in.
Diet: Trees

Information: By the end of the Cretaceous, the only important sauropods belonged to the titanosaur group. They mainly lived in the southern continents and many of them had backs covered in armor.

CAUDIPTERYX

Meaning: *Wing tail*
Time: Early Cretaceous
Size: 2 ft. 3 in.
Diet: Insects

Information: One of the small theropods that show distinctive bird features. It was very lightly built and had feathers on the wings and the tail. However, the wings were too small to allow it to fly. Here it is shown in the bottom, right of the picture.

VELOCIRAPTOR

Meaning: *Fast hunter*
Time: Late Cretaceous
Size: 6 ft. 6 in.
Diet: Other dinosaurs
Information: One of the most well-known, small, hunting dinosaurs. It was also very bird like, and its main weapon was its killing claw on its foot. It probably hunted in packs.

TYRANNOSAURUS

Meaning: *Tyrant lizard*
Time: Late Cretaceous
Size: 32 ft. 8 in.
Diet: Other dinosaurs
Information: Once regarded as the biggest of the meat-eating dinosaurs, it is certainly still the most widely known, with its huge head and its steak-knife teeth as big as bananas. How the tiny arms were used is still a mystery.

Oviraptor

Time: Late Cretaceous

Diet: Not known, maybe eggs

Habitat: Open country

Information: Small theropod with a heavy bird-like bill.

Spinosaurus

Time: Late Cretaceous

Diet: Other dinosaurs

Habitat: Open country

Information: Had a large fin on its back.

Masiakasaurus

Time: Late Cretaceous

Diet: Fish

Habitat: Riversides

Information: A snaggle-toothed fish-hunting abelisaur.

Troodon

Time: Late Cretaceous

Diet: Smaller animals

Habitat: Woodlands

Information: A big-eyed fast hunter, probably the most intelligent of dinosaurs.

Sinosauropteryx

Time: Early Cretaceous

Diet: Insects and small animals

Habitat: Lakesides

Information: A typical tiny theropod, but covered in feathers.

THERIZINOSAURUS

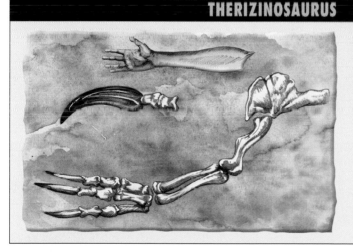

Meaning: *Scythe lizard*
Time: Late Cretaceous
Size: 26 ft. 2 in.
Diet: Plants
Information: *Thorizinosaurus* was the biggest of the therizinosaurs. It had big arms with the largest claws of any dinosaur. Claw bones measuring 2 ft. 3 in. have been unearthed. They may have been used for pulling down branches to reach feed on the leaves.

CARNOTAURUS

Meaning: *Flesh-eating bull*
Time: Late Cretaceous
Size: 32 ft. 8 in.
Diet: Other dinosaurs
Information: While the tyrannosaurs were the biggest meat-eaters of North America, another group, the *abelisaurs*, were the largest carnivores in the southern continents. *Carnotaurus*, with its bull-like horns, was a typical abelisaur.

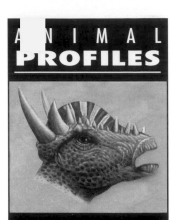

Stygimoloch

Time: Late Cretaceous

Diet: Low vegetation

Habitat: Open woodland

Information: Bone-headed dinosaur with a spectacular array of horns.

Corythosaurus

Time: Late Cretaceous

Diet: Trees

Habitat: Woodland

Information: Duckbill with a semicircular crest.

Anatotitan

Time: Late Cretaceous

Diet: Trees

Habitat: Woodland

Information: One of the duckbills that had no crest.

Polacanthus

Time: Early Cretaceous

Diet: Low vegetation

Habitat: Open woodland

Information: An early ankylosaur.

Tsintaosaurus

Time: Early Cretaceous

Diet: Trees

Habitat: Woodland

Information: Duckbill with a single spike for a crest.

Ouranosaurus

Time: Early Cretaceous

Diet: Trees

Habitat: Open woodland

Information: A sail-backed relative of *Iguanodon*.

CRETACEOUS LIFE

With the wide range of landscapes and plant types that existed in the Cretaceous, an equally wide range of plant-eating dinosaurs, mostly ornithischians, evolved to make the best use of it. When we think of dinosaurs, we tend to think of saurischians. However, it was the ornithischian types that flourished at this time, with many more species than the saurischians.

NEW PLANTS

Flowering plants producing seeds appeared in early Cretaceous times and spread rapidly at the end of the period. Possible reasons include:

Magnolia

Oak

Willow

Birch

- Dinosaurs put such pressure on plant life that they evolved quick-growing seeds to repair the damage.

- Increasing temperatures toward the end of the period encouraged tougher seeds.

- By the end of the period, there were many familiar plants, and the landscape began to look like it does today. However, grass had yet to evolve. No actual fossil flowers have been found, but scientists can work out what

species might have flourished by looking at fossils of seeds, leaves, wood, and pollen grains.

VARIED HABITATS

Different plants live in different places. It is possible that the new plants flourished on the well-watered lowlands, while the old plants, such as cycads and old-style conifers, continued in the hills. The typical Cretaceous plant-eaters, evolved to tackle the new food, would have lived on the lowlands, while the older types, like the waning sauropods, would have remained in the hills.

***Saltasaurus* was a sauropod.**

• See page 36 for more information on SALTASAURUS.

EUOPLOCEPHALUS

Meaning: *Well-armored head*
Time: Late Cretaceous
Size: 19ft. 7 in.
Diet: Low-growing vegetation
Information: The ankylosaurs took over from the stegosaurs as the armored dinosaurs of the Cretaceous period. There were three families — the primitive polacanthids, the ankylosaurids such as *Euoplocephalus* with clubs on the ends of their tails, and the nodosaurids that had spikes on their shoulders.

IGUANODON

Meaning: *Iguana tooth*
Time: Early Cretaceous
Size: 32 ft. 8 in.
Diet: Trees and low-growing vegetation
Information: *Iguanodon* was one of the first dinosaurs to be discovered.

A complex chewing action with jawbones that moved in relation to each other, batteries of grinding teeth, and cheeks to hold the food, meant that this dinosaur could eat all kinds of plant food.

PARASAUROLOPHUS

Meaning: *Like a lizard crest*
Time: Late Cretaceous
Size: 32 ft. 8 in.
Diet: Trees and low-growing vegetation.
Information: *Parasaurolophus* was one of the duckbilled dinosaurs, which evolved from animals such as Iguanodons. This group spread to become the most important plant-eating animals of the northern hemisphere at the end of the Cretaceous. Many had crests on their heads.

TRICERATOPS

Meaning: *Three-horned head*
Time: Late Cretaceous
Size: 26 ft. 2 in.
Diet: Bushes and low-growing vegetation.
Information: *Triceratops* was part of a group of horned dinosaurs called *ceratopsians*. This group evolved from small, rabbit-sized animals at the beginning of the Cretaceous to rhinoceros-sized beasts with heavy shields on their heads by the end of the period.

ANIMAL PROFILES

Edmontonia
Time: Late Cretaceous
Diet: Low vegetation
Habitat: Open woodland
Information: A typical nodosaurid ankylosaur.

Struthiosaurus
Time: Late Cretaceous
Diet: Low vegetation
Habitat: Islands
Information: A dwarf nodosaurid ankylosaur.

Ankylosaurus
Time: Late Cretaceous
Diet: Low vegetation
Habitat: Open woodland
Information: The biggest of the ankylosaurid ankylosaurs.

Styracosaurus
Time: Late Cretaceous
Diet: Low vegetation
Habitat: Open plains
Information: Horned dinosaur with a single horn and spikes around the neck.

Psittacosaurus
Time: Early Cretaceous
Diet: Plants and small animals
Habitat: Desert-like scrubland
Information: *Psittacosaurus* was around for 40 million years: the longest-lived type of dinosaur.

Archaeoceratops
Time: Early Cretaceous
Diet: Low vegetation
Habitat: Desert
Information: Small ancestral horned dinosaur.

39

THE GREAT EXTIN-TION

At the end of the Cretaceous period—which is also the end of the Mesozoic era—there was a great extinction. It was not the only mass-extinction to have taken place in the Earth's history, or even the greatest. However, it does seem to be the one that has caught everybody's imagination. Not only did it wipe out the dinosaurs, but it also took the pterosaurs and the great sea reptiles of the time.

DISEASES

As the continents continued to move and the sea levels fluctuated, land bridges began to open up between one continent and another. Animals of one continent would have been free to migrate to another and live with the animals there. These newcomers would have brought diseases that they were immune to, but the local population would not be. Exchange of diseases like this would have weakened the populations so much that extinction would have followed.

Evidence

The mass extinction in the oceans seems to have taken place anywhere up to half a million years before that on land, suggesting that something immediate and catastrophic like a meteorite impact was not to blame. The largest animals of the world were affected, something that we see today if plagues spread through natural populations.

WHAT CAUSED THE GREAT EXTINCTION?

Scientists are still not sure what led to the catastrophic loss of life at the end of the Cretaceous, but there are several serious possibilities:

Meteorite or comet strike

Volcanic activity

Changing climates

Diseases

Many palaeontologists believe a combination of all of these factors wiped out the dinosaurs.

METEORITE OR COMET STRIKE

The most popular theory is that a body from space struck the Earth 65 million years ago. This would have had several effects.

- Shock waves would have killed everything in the vicinity.

- Seismic sea waves, called *tsunamis*, would have flooded all the lowlands.

- Hot molten debris would have caused widespread wildfires.

- Clouds of dust would have cut off the sunshine, causing short-term global cooling.

This disrupted atmosphere would have produced a long-term greenhouse effect.

Evidence
- A buried formation looking like a meteorite crater of the right size and age has been found in Yucatan in Mexico.

- Sedimentary rocks have been discovered in Texas that look like tsunami deposits.

- Deposits of the element iridium, only found abundantly in meteorites or beneath the Earth's crust, have been detected in a layer all over the world.

- Deposits of quartz crystals have been unearthed that show signs of being deformed by a heavy impact.

CHANGING CLIMATES

The dinosaurs and the other big animals may have become so well adapted to the habitable climates of the Mesozoic Era that they did not have the capability to cope with any dramatic change.

Evidence
- The end of the Cretaceous period shows signs of increasing temperatures.
- Dinosaur eggshells of the time show signs of weakening — evidence of heat stress.
- There have been observations of changing sea levels of the time that would influence climates.
- Replacement of tropical forest with temperate woodland took place, indicating a sudden cooling after the increasing temperatures.

A COMBINATION OF ALL OF THESE

There seems to be evidence that the dinosaurs were fading in the last few million years of the Cretaceous.

If this is so, then a meteorite impact could have finished them off.

The Yucatan impact site at the time was exactly at the other side of the world from the area of the Deccan Trapps. Perhaps the two are linked. The impact in Yucatan could have set up vibrations through the Earth that focused on the other side and generated the volcanic activity.

Perhaps the meteor broke in two, one part hitting Yucatan and the other hitting India 12 hours later, inducing the vulcanism. Disease and plague would inevitably spread through populations weakened by natural disaster.

VOLCANIC ACTIVITY

Widespread volcanic activity would put so much debris and gas into the atmosphere that the climates would change — in the same way as would be caused by a meteorite impact. The deposits of iridium could have been brought to the Earth's surface by volcanoes.

Evidence
Half of the sub-continent of India is made up of basaltic lava flows, called the *Deccan Trapps*, that erupted at the end of the Cretaceous period, 65 million years ago, which could have wiped out the entire dinosaur population.

WINNERS AND LOSERS

The exinction event wiped out significant percentages of species of most groups.

From this chart we see that mammals and birds were heavily affected. They were, however, small, adaptable, and recovered quickly.

Throughout the Mesozoic, mammals had been small, shrew-like, and insignificant. This was about to change.

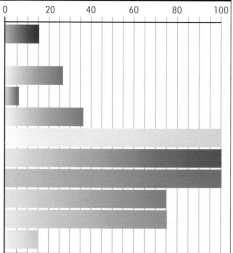

Fish 15%
Amphibians 0%
Tortoises and turtles 27%
Lizards and snakes 6%
Crocodiles 36%
Dinosaurs 100%
Pterosaurus 100%
Plesiosaurs 100%
Birds 75%
Marsupial mammals 75%
Placental mammals 14%

REPENOMAMUS

Meaning: *Fearsome mammal*
Time: Early Cretaceous
Size: 3 ft. 3 in.
Diet: Dinosaurs
Information: Found in lake deposits in China, this dog-sized mammal had the bones of small dinosaurs in its stomach.

EARLY TERTIARY PERIOD

TERTIARY TIMELINE

65–1.8 MYA

Tertiary Period	Neogene	Pliocene
		Miocene
	Palaeogene	Oligocene
		Eocene
		Paleocene

ANIMAL PROFILES

Indricotherium
Time: Oligocene

Diet: Trees

Habitat: Woodland

Information: A gigantic rhinoceros. The biggest land animal known.

Ambulocetus
Time: Eocene

Diet: Meat

Habitat: Shallow seas

Information: The earliest-known whale. Swam like a sea lion.

Uintatherium
Time: Eocene

Diet: Leaves

Habitat: Forests

Information: One of the various big rhinoceros-like mammals.

Leptictidium
Time: Eocene

Diet: Insects

Habitat: Shallow seas

Information: Swift, long-legged little insectivore.

After the Great Extinction, Earth looked much like it did before, with moderate climates and thick forest over most of the land. The animals have greatly changed, though. With the big reptiles gone, the Age of Mammals was about to begin. This age included the eventual evolution of the first hominid.

THE WORLD IN THE EARLY TERTIARY PERIOD

By this period, the continents of the world had moved into an almost recognizable form. The major differences in the image below are that Australia had recently broken away from Antarctica and was beginning its long trek northwards towards the equator, and India was still an island moving across the Indian Ocean from Africa.

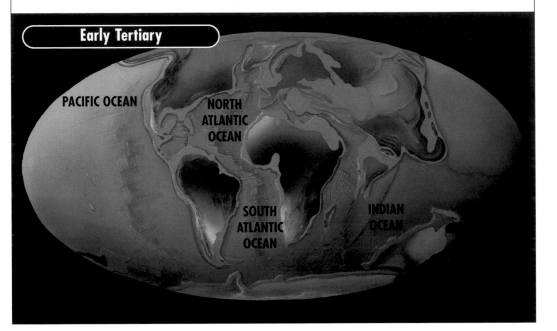

Early Tertiary

PACIFIC OCEAN

NORTH ATLANTIC OCEAN

SOUTH ATLANTIC OCEAN

INDIAN OCEAN

PLANT AND ANIMAL LIFE

The plant life is similar to that of the late Cretaceous, with thick forests of modern type plants.

There is still not much in the way of grass. Animal life has been taken over by mammals.

- On the land, replacing the dinosaurs.
- In the sea, replacing the plesiosaurs and mosasaurs.
- In the air, replacing the pterosaurs.
- Birds are also important. At the beginning of the period, there are flightless birds that are like their dinosaur ancestors. These birds are the main predators of the time.

MEANING OF THE NAME

The word *tertiary* comes from an old Victorian dating system.

Primary — The Precambrian and the Palaeozoic.

Secondary — The Mesozoic.

Tertiary — From the end of the dinosaurs to the Ice Age.

Quaternary — The Ice Age and the present day.

The last two terms are still used. The Tertiary is divided into the early Tertiary, called the *Palaeogene*, and the late Tertiary, called the *Neogene*.

MAMMAL NAMES

Many mammal names end with *-therium*, an old Greek name for *beast*, just like many dinosaur names end with *-saurus*, an old Greek name for *lizard*.

BRONTOTHERIUM

Meaning: *Thunder beast*
Time: Oligocene
Size: 6 ft. 6in. tall
Diet: Low vegetation
Information: Many of the larger mammals, such as *Brontotherium*, developed with big bodies to digest plants and horns on the head for defence.

ANIMAL PROFILES

Icaronycteris
Time: Eocene

Diet: Insects

Habitat: Trees

Information: The earliest bats were almost identical to modern bats.

Hypsodus
Time: Eocene

Diet: Seeds and fruits

Habitat: Treetops

Information: A short-legged squirrel-like climber.

Chriacus
Time: Eocene

Diet: Fruits, insects and small animals

Habitat: Undergrowth

Information: A generalized mammal with front limbs adapted for digging.

Buxolostos
Time: Eocene

Diet: Shellfish

Habitat: Lakes

Information: An otter-like swimming mammal with strong teeth.

Presbyornis
Time: Eocene

Diet: Small things in the mud

Habitat: Lakes

Info: A long-legged duck.

Plesiadapis
Time: Paleocene

Diet: Leaves

Habitat: Trees

Information: An early member of the primate group, like a lemur.

HYRACOTHERIUM

Meaning: *Hyrax beast*
Time: Eocene
Size: 1 ft. 6 in. long
Diet: Leaves
Information: *Hyracotherium* was the earliest member of the horse family. It was only the size of a rabbit and had teeth for chewing leaves from bushes, not grass from the ground.

DIATRYMA

Time: Paleocene to Eocene
Size: 6 ft. 6 in. tall
Diet: Mammals
Information: With the lack of carnivores around, some birds become the main hunters, taking on the appearance of their dinosaur ancestors. *Diatryma* is an example of such a bird.

OXYAENA

Meaning: *Sharp claw*
Time: Eocene
Size: 1 ft. 6 in. long
Diet: Small animals
Information: The meat-eating mammals became established with the creodonts, which were similar in appearance but unrelated to modern carnivores.

Neohipparion
Time: Miocene

Diet: Grass

Habitat: Grasslands

Information: The horses are now plains animals, with grass-eating teeth.

Alticamelus
Time: Miocene

Diet: Leaves

Habitat: Woods

Information: Camel with a long giraffe-like neck.

Megantereon
Time: Miocene

Diet: Big animals

Habitat: Grasslands

Information: The true cats were beginning to evolve, including some with big teeth.

Paleoparadoxia
Time: Miocene

Diet: Seaweed or shellfish

Habitat: Shorelines

Information: A massive amphibious mammal that may have lived like a walrus.

Cranioceras
Time: Miocene

Diet: Leaves

Habitat: Subtropical woodland

Information: A deer-like hoofed mammal with third horn that grew up and back from the rear of the skull that was used for fighting.

LATE TERTIARY PERIOD

During this period, the Earth's appearance began to change dramatically. The forests died away as grasslands spread everywhere. This was caused by a general cooling of the climate. The open plains encouraged the evolution of a new kind of animal—animals with long legs, that they used for running over wide expanses, and specialized digestive systems for breaking down the grass they ate.

THE WORLD IN THE LATE TERTIARY PERIOD

The late Tertiary period has taken on a very familiar appearance. The main differences between it and the present day is that North America is still separated from South America, and a large area of sea and island chains is in southern Europe. This sea area is the result of the continent of Africa moving toward Europe and creating the Alps from the intervening marine sediments as it goes.

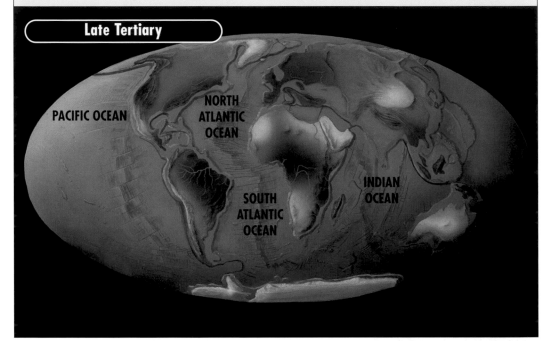

Late Tertiary

PACIFIC OCEAN

NORTH ATLANTIC OCEAN

SOUTH ATLANTIC OCEAN

INDIAN OCEAN

PHORUSRHACOS

Meaning: *Terror bird*
Time: Miocene
Size: 8 ft. 2 in. tall
Diet: Large animals
Information: South America, still isolated from North America, had all kinds of strange animals that existed nowhere else in the world. *Phorusrhacos* was a fast runner and could outrun most of its prey.

THE COMING OF GRASS

The evolutionary advantage of grass is that the main part of its growing stem lies underground.
The exposed leaves can be eaten by grazing animals or burnt by fire, but the main part is protected in the soil. This makes it ideal for open areas in very dry climates.

The tough leaves, full of silica, require extra hard teeth and complex digestive systems to eat it.

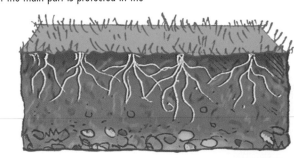

DEINOTHERIUM

Meaning: *Terrible beast*
Time: Miocene to Pliocene
Size: 6 ft. 6 in. tall
Diet: Ground plants

Information: Many kinds of elephant established themselves at this time. *Deinotherium* had tusks pointing down on the lower jaw.

SYNTHETOCERAS

Meaning: *Fused horn*
Time: Miocene
Size: 4 ft. 9 in. long
Diet: Grass
Information: Typical grass-eating animals, like the *Synthetoceras*, living on plains have long faces, placing their eyes high up on their head, allowing them to see danger coming from a long way away. They also had long legs so that they can run away from danger.

SIVATHERIUM

Meaning: *Beast of Siva*
Time: Pliocene
Size: 6 ft. 6 in. long
Diet: Ground plants
Information: The giraffe species were more important during the Tertiary than they are now. Many groups thrived between the Miocene and the recent past. All of these groups had bony horns, called *ossicones*. *Sivatherium* was an early example of these early giraffes, with a massive body and a huge set of horns. However, it looked more like a deer than a giraffe.

COOLING CLIMATE

Throughout the history of the Earth, we have noted fluctuating atmospheric temperatures, producing changing climates. Toward the end of the Tertiary, there is a distinct cooling off.

TODAY
PLEISTOCENE
TERTIARY
CRETACEOUS
JURASSIC
TRIASSIC
PERMIAN
CARBONIFEROUS
DEVONIAN
SILURIAN
ORDOVICIAN
CAMBRIAN
PRECAMBRIAN

COOL — WARM — COOL — WARM — COOL — WARM — COOL — WARM — COOL

72°F   63°F   54°F

ANIMAL PROFILES

Thylacosmilus
Time: Pliocene
Diet: Big animals
Habitat: Grasslands
Information: A South American marsupial that looked like and lived like a sabre-toothed tiger.

Platybelodon
Time: Miocene and Pliocene
Diet: Leaves, grasses, bark
Habitat: Grasslands, forests
Information: Elephant with shovel-like tusks.

Epigaulus
Time: Miocene
Diet: Roots and tubers
Habitat: Grasslands
Information: A burrowing horned rodent.

Dimylus
Time: Miocene
Diet: Insects and small water animals
Habitat: Rivers
Information: A small aquatic insectivore, like a desman.

Daphoneus
Time: Miocene
Diet: Small animals, carrion and plants
Habitat: Plains
Information: A relative of the dog, that lived like a bear.

Eurhinodelphis
Time: Miocene
Diet: Fish
Habitat: Open ocean
Information: A dolphin with a swordfish-like snout.

QUATERNARY PERIOD

The cooling experienced at the end of the late Tertiary period becomes extreme, as the world slips into the last ice age. As the ice caps spread outward from the poles and downwards from the mountain tops, altering the climate throughout the world, the animal life changes to adapt to these harsh new conditions.

THE WORLD IN THE QUATERNARY PERIOD

The map of the world in the Ice Age shows how much of it was covered in glaciers. Apart from that there seems to be some difference in the coastline, especially around the southern tip of South America and the East Indies. The ice caps have absorbed so much of the ocean's water that the sea level is much lower everywhere, exposing wide areas of continental shelf.

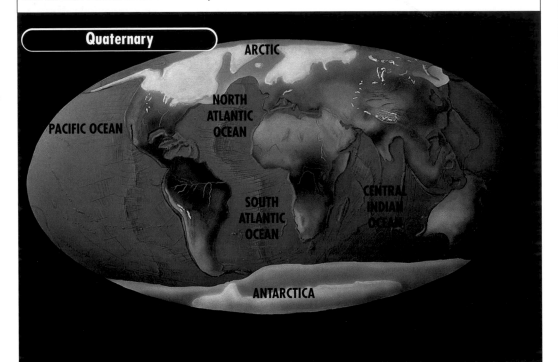

Quaternary

ARCTIC

NORTH ATLANTIC OCEAN

PACIFIC OCEAN

SOUTH ATLANTIC OCEAN

CENTRAL INDIAN OCEAN

ANTARCTICA

CAUSES OF THE ICE AGE

There are several possible events that caused the last Ice Age:

- Wobble of the Earth's axis.
- Variation in the Earth's orbit, affecting the amount of sunlight received.
- Joining of North and South America closing off the seaway between the warm Pacific and the Atlantic. This made the Atlantic colder and affected the polar ice cap.

MEANING OF THE NAME

The fourth division of geological time, as devised by the Victorians. • See page 43

AGES OF THE QUATERNARY

Most of the period is the Pleistocene epoch, also called the *Ice Age*. The rest is the Holocene, or the present day, which occupies about the last ten thousand years.

GLACIAL STAGES

The Ice Age was not a single continuous cold snap. There were glacial periods when the ice was at its most extensive, and interglacial periods when the climate was warm — often warmer than it is now.

GLACIALS (Europe)

Würm	125,000 to 10,000 years ago
Riss	360,000 to 235,000 years ago
Mindel	7,800,000 to 670,000 years ago
Gunz	1.15 million to 900,000 years ago
Donau	1.6 million to 1.37 million years ago

GLACIALS (North America)

Wisonsinian	30,000 to 8,000 years ago
Illinoian	300,000 to 130,000 years ago
Several ill-defined pre-Illinoian	2.5 million to 500,000 years ago

Ocean sediment studies show that there were many fine divisions within these glaciation events.

EVIDENCE OF GLACIATION

Landforms dating from the time
(*Clockwise from top left*)

- Striations (deep scratches on solid rock surfaces)

- Moraine (heaps of debris carried and deposited by glaciers)

- Kettle holes (lakes formed where an abandoned lump of glacier melted)

- Raised beaches (formed by higher sea level when the local area was pushed down by the weight of the ice cover)

Biological evidence
- Pollen of cold-adapted plants found in lake deposits of the time.

- Skeletons of cold-adapted animals.

Glyptodon
Time: Pleistocene

Diet: Low plants

Habitat: Grassland

Information: A giant armadillo-like animal from South America.

Coelodonta
Time: Pleistocene

Diet: Grass and moss

Habitat: Tundra

Information: The woolly rhinoceros.

Megaceros
Time: Pleistocene

Diet: Grass and moss

Habitat: Tundra

Information: A giant elk with a large spread of horns.

Diprodoton
Time: Pleistocene

Diet: Grass and moss

Habitat: Grassland

Information: Part of the fauna of isolated Australia, like a giant wombat.

Megalania
Time: Pleistocene

Diet: Big animals

Habitat: Desert

Information: A giant monitor lizard.

SMILODON

Meaning: *Saber tooth*
Time: Pleistocene
Size: 6 ft. 6 in. long
Diet: Big mammals
Information: The saber-toothed tiger evolved to be able to prey on the big plant-eaters of the time.

ELEPHAS PRIMIGENIUS

Time: *Pleistocene*
Size: 6 ft. 6 in. tall
Diet: Ground plants
Information: The woolly mammoth was typical of the big animals of the time. It developed deposits of fat and a shaggy coat to protect against the cold.

MEGATHERIUM

Meaning: *Big beast*
Time: Pleistocene
Size: 9 ft. 8 in. tall
Diet: Trees
Information: Several types of giant ground sloth existed at the time, evolving in South America but spreading to North America as the Central American isthmus was established.

MACRAUCHENIA

Meaning: *Big llama*
Time: Pleistocene
Size: 6 ft. 6 in. tall
Diet: Ground plants
Information: The isolated South America still provided a home to some strange beasts. *Macrauchenia* was a long-legged, long-necked animal with a trunk.

THE FIRST HUMAN BEINGS

The appearance of first human beings is a relatively new development in Earth's history. From our remote ancestors, the unicellular Precambrian organisms, we can trace our ancestry from fish, amphibians, mammal-like reptiles, primitive shrew-like mammals, lemur-like early primates, monkey-like forms, and the ape-like forms to, finally, a stage where distinctive human features begin to appear. These features include upright posture, nimble hands, and the ability to make and use tools.

Australopithecus africanus

Time: Pliocene. 3–2.3 million years ago

Diet: Omnivorous

Habitat: Open grassland

Information: The first human beings to be found, in 1924.

Australopithecus anamensis

Time: Pliocene. 4.2–3.9 million years ago

Diet: Omnivorous

Habitat: Open grassland

Information: The earliest-known *Australopithecus* species.

Australopithecus afarensis

Time: Pliocene. 4–2.75 million years ago

Diet: Omnivorous

Habitat: Open grassland

Information: Known as *Lucy*. Still with ape-like jaw and fingers.

Australopithecus bahrelghazali

Time: Pliocene

Diet: Omnivorous

Habitat: Open grassland

Information: 3.5–3 million years ago. More modern jaw than *Australopithecus afarensis*.

WHEN AND WHERE DID HUMAN BEINGS FIRST APPEAR?

From fossils, scientists have discovered that the first human-like mammals lived on the eastern side of Africa at the beginning of the Pleistocene.

Homo erectus

Ardipthecus ramidus
Australopithecus afarenis
Homo sapiens?

Australopithecus bahrelghazali

Orrorin
Kenyanthropus

Australopithecus anamensis
Australopithecus afarensis
Australopithecus boisei
Australopithecus aethiopicus
Homo erectus
Homo habilis
Homo rudolfensis

Australopithecus africanus
Australopithecus robustus
Homo habilis

WHY DID WE STAND UPRIGHT?

The upright stance is probably due to

- Fewer trees with the onset of the ice age, forcing ape-like animals to live closer to the ground.

- Tall grasses created the need to see over them.

- A vertical animal would be less susceptible to sunburn than one down on all fours with less surface directly hit by the sun.

- Hands that were once used for climbing in branches would now be free for other purposes.

- Brain at the top of a vertical spinal column would have a better chance to enlarge than one at the end of a horizontal one.

ANIMAL PROFILES

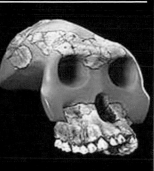

Australopithecus garhi
Time: Pliocene. 2.5 million years ago

Diet: Omnivorous

Habitat: Open grassland

Information: Possibly a tool-user.

Australopithecus aethiopicus
Time: Pliocene. 2.5 million years ago

Diet: Omnivorous – tough, grainy foods

Habitat: Open grassland

Information: This species is known as the *Black Skull*; as one fossil absorbed minerals during fossilization, giving it a black color.

Australopithecus robustus
Time: Pleistocene. 1.8–1.5 million years ago

Diet: Plants

Habitat: Open grassland

Information: A heavily-built species with muscular jaws and a flat face.

Australopithecus boisei
Time: Pliocene to Pleistocene. 2.3–1.4 million years ago

Diet: Plants

Habitat: Open grassland

Information: Very large jaws and teeth, nicknamed "nutcracker man."

- See page 55 for more information on *LOUIS SEYMOUR BAZETT LEAKY* who discovered Australopithecus.

ORRORIN

Meaning: *Original man*
Time: Miocene. Dating from about 6 million years ago
Size: 3 ft. 3 in. tall
Diet: Omnivorous
Information: The primate that seems to represent the split between the ape lineage and the human lineage.

ARDIPITHECUS

Meaning: *Ground ape*
Time: Pliocene. 4.4 million years ago
Size: 3 ft. 3 in. tall
Diet: Omnivorous
Information: Better-known than the older *Orrorin* and more widely regarded as the oldest hominid.

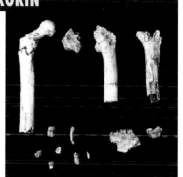

KENYANTHROPUS

Meaning: *Kenyan ape*
Time: Pliocene. 3.5–3.3 million years ago
Size: 3 ft. 3 in. tall
Diet: Omnivorous
Information: An offshoot from the hominid line, with a mixture of primitive (small ear holes) and advanced (flat face and small teeth).

AUSTRALOPITHECUS

Meaning: *Southern ape*
Time: Pliocene to Pleistocene
Size: 3 ft. 3 in. tall
Diet: Omnivorous
Information: The most important of our immediate ancestors. Consisting of several species, one would have been our direct ancestor.

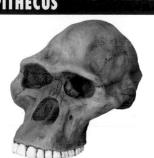

THE GENUS *HOMO*

The events of the past did not just happen to reach the present day. Although we like to think that the Earth's history has happened so that humans can exist, humans are just another step in the development of life. Progress will continue, and the exciting drama of life on Earth will continue as long as the Earth itself exists. Who knows what exciting events could happen on Earth in future years to come?

Homo habilis
Time: Pliocene. 2.3–1.6 million years ago

Diet: Omnivorous

Habitat: Open grassland

Information: A toolmaker and contemporary of *Australopithecus africanus*.

Homo erectus
Time: Pleistocene. 1.8–0.3 million years ago

Diet: Omnivorous

Habitat: Everywhere

Information: The earliest widespread species, from France to Java, representing the move out of Africa.

Homo ergaster
Time: Pliocene. 1.8–1.2 million years ago

Diet: Omnivorous

Habitat: Open grassland

Information: Very similar to *Homo erectus*, but confined to Africa.

Homo heidelbergensis
Time: Pleistocene. 0.5–0.2 million years ago

Diet: Omnivorous

Habitat: Open grassland

Information: Intermediate between *Homo erectus* and *Homo sapiens* and sometimes classed as one or the other.

OUT OF THE CRADLE

All the early evolution of hominids took place in Africa. It was with the development of *Homo erectus* that they left Africa and spread through Europe and Asia. Then, evolving into *Homo sapiens*, they traveled to other parts of Earth.

Australia	65,000 years ago
North America	50,000 years ago
South America	12,500 years ago

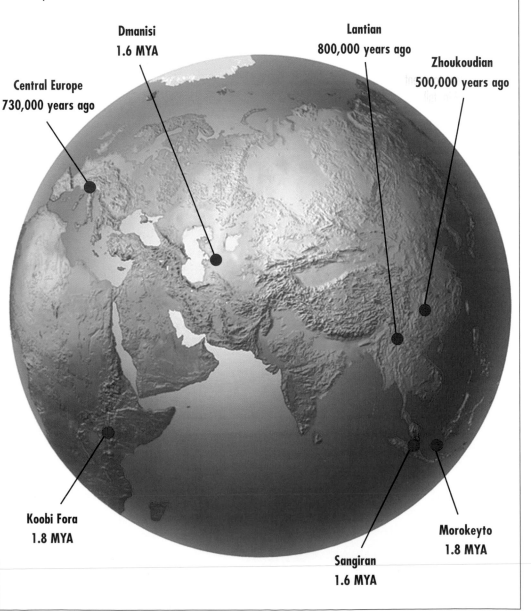

Dmanisi 1.6 MYA

Lantian 800,000 years ago

Zhoukoudian 500,000 years ago

Central Europe 730,000 years ago

Koobi Fora 1.8 MYA

Sangiran 1.6 MYA

Morokeyto 1.8 MYA

THE DEVELOPMENT OF CULTURE AND CIVILIZATION

Things that we take for granted in civilized life developed over a long period of time, and in different places at different times.

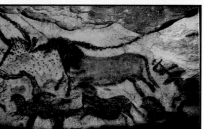

Neolithic (*new stone age*)
Development of agriculture, everywhere   9,000–1,800 years ago

Hunting weapons, North America   11,000 years ago

Upper Palaeolithic (*old stone age*)
Cave art, France   33,000 years ago

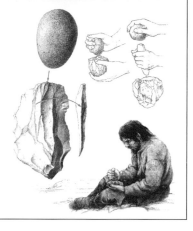

Lower Palaeolithic
Complex flake tools, France   100,000–40,000 years ago

Simple flake tools, Britain and France   450,000–100,000 years ago

Stone tools, everywhere   2.5–1.5 million years ago

HOMO

Time: Pliocene to recent
Size: 5 ft. 9 in. tall
Diet: Omnivorous
Information: The modern human being. Several species developed, but only one survived.

UNCOVERING THE PREHISTORIC WORLD

The history of life on Earth is pieced together through the detailed accumulation of knowledge gained over the centuries by visionary and hard-working scientists. A list such as this cannot be exhaustive. There are many others whose contributions were as great but just did not make it on to this page because of lack of room.

TIMELINE OF THE HISTORY OF GEOLOGY AND PALAEONTOLOGY

610–425 BC Philosophers Thales, Anaximander, Pythagoras, Xenophanes, and Herodotus recognize that fossils show that the distribution of land and sea was once different.

Calcite – a common mineral

78 BC Pliny the Elder writes the first natural history encyclopaedia.

c AD 1000 Al-Beruni (973–1050) observes that different grades of sediment is deposited by different strengths of river currents—an early observation of sedimentology. He also puts precious minerals into geological context.

1020 Avicenna (or Sina) observes the work of erosion.

1056 Albertus Magnus publishes a book on minerals.

1500 Leonardo da Vinci states that fossils are remains of animals and their enclosing rocks must have been lifted from below sea level.

1542 Leonhart Fuchs publishes a catalog of 500 plant species.

1546 Georgius Agricola (born George Bauer, 1494–1555), "Father of mineralogy," classifies minerals by their crystal shape and composition. Publishes an analysis of ore bodies.

1585 Michele Mercati opens the first geological museum.

1596 Dutch cartographer Abraham Ortelius first suggests continental drift.

1600 William Gilbert, Elizabeth I's physician, describes the Earth's magnetism.

1616 Italian philosopher Lucilio Vanini first to suggest humans descended from apes. He was executed for this belief.

1641 Lawyer Isaac La Peyrère suggests that people existed before Adam and Eve. His ideas were only published after his death.

James Cook

1658 Jesuit missionary Martino Martini shows that Chinese history predates the above. Nobody takes notice.

1668 Robert Hooke claims that Earth's movements, and not the biblical Flood, moved fossils to dry land.

1669 Nicolaus Steno (born Neils Stensen, 1638–86) establishes the laws of stratigraphy, which state that rock beds laid down horizontally, stacked on one another, and subsequently contorted.

1679 Scandinavian historian Olof Rudbeck tries to date sedimentary rocks.

1688 The Ashmolean Museum opens in Oxford—the world's first public museum.

1715 Edmund Halley suggests the age of the Earth can be calculated from the salinity of the seas.

1735 Linnaeus establishes the binomial classification of living things.

1745 Mikhail Vasil'evich Lomonosov (1711–65) recognizes that ancient geological processes would have been similar to today's, in anticipation of James Hutton (see **1795**).

1749 Georges-Louis Leclerc de Buffon speculates that the planets formed by a comet crashing into the sun. The people in power force him to retract it.

1751 Diderot and d'Alembert publish the first encyclopaedia—with a reliance on factual information rather than on traditional beliefs.

1760 Giovanni Arduino classifies the geological column – Primary: with no fossils, Secondary: deformed and with fossils, Tertiary: horizontal and with fossils, and Quaternary: loose sands and gravels over the rest. This was a rough basis of modern classification.

1766 Torbern Olaf Bergman (1735–1784) sees that different rock types were formed at different times and appreciates the organic origin of fossils.

1768 James Cook's voyage brings an awareness of the range of plants and animals around the world to the United Kingdom.

The Earth's magnetism

1771 Joseph Priestley discovers oxygen and shows its importance to life.

1778 Buffon puts the age of the Earth at 74,832 years.

1789 French researcher Antoine Lavoisier interprets different sedimentary rocks as showing different sea levels in the past.

1795 James Hutton, the "Founder of modern geology," sees geological processes as a cycle, with no beginning and no end.

1799 Alexander von Humboldt names the Jurassic system.

1799 British surveyor William Smith produces the first geological map, establishing the importance of fossils to define rocks and times.

1804 Cuvier acknowledges that fossil animals are older than can be explained by the Bible and suggests previous cycles of creation and destruction.

Alfred Wegener

1824 Buckland describes the first dinosaur.

1830 Charles Lyell publishes his influential *Principles of Geology*.

1837 Charles Darwin uses natural selection to explain evolution, but the idea is not published until 1859.

1837 Swiss scientist Louis Agassiz detects the Ice Age.

1841 William Smith's nephew, John Phillips, names the geological eras *Palaeozoic*, *Mesozoic*, and *Cenozoic*.

1842 Sir Richard Owen invents the term *dinosaur*.

1848 Science magazine established by the American Association for the Advancement of Science.

1866 Austrian monk Gregor Mendel establishes the laws of heredity. His work remains unknown until about 1900.

1871 Darwin publishes *The Descent of Man*.

1894 Eugene Debois describes *Pithecanthus erectus* (now *Homo erectus*) as the missing link between humans and apes.

1902 Walter Sutton discovers the *chromosome theory of inheritance*.

1902 Physicist Ernest Rutherford shows that radioactivity means that the Earth is older than Kelvin said.

1912 Alfred Wegener proposes *continental drift*.

1927 Belgian priest Georges Lemaître proposes that the universe began with the explosion of a primeval atom—a forerunner of the Big Bang theory.

1934 American geologist Charles F. Richter establishes the Richter scale for measuring earthquakes.

1946 Geologist Reg Sprigg finds the oldest fossils of multicellular organisms in Australia.

Crick and Watson

1953 Stanley Miller and Harold Urey combine the gases of the Earth's initial atmosphere and form the chemicals from which living things are made.

1953 James Watson and Francis Crick determine the molecular structure of DNA.

1953 Fiesel Houtermans and Claire Patterson use radiometric dating to date the Earth at 4.5 billion years old.

1956 Keith Runcorn notes polar wandering based on paleomagnetic studies.

Darwin studied the features of different species to develop his theory of evolution.

1961 Amateur meteorologist GS Callander notes the rise in greenhouse gases in the atmosphere and warns of a global warming.

1963 Fred Vine and Drummond Matthews discover *seafloor spreading*. This leads to the establishment of *plate tectonics*.

1964 Arno Penzias and Robert Wilson detect cosmic radiation and use it to confirm the Big Bang Theory.

1966 Willi Hennig develops *cladistics*, a new approach to studying evolutionary relationships.

1969 Moon rock samples prove that the moon the same age as the Earth.

1972 Stephen Jay Gould and Niles Eldredge develop the theory of *punctuated equilibrium*, meaning that evolution takes place in short bursts.

1974 John Ostrom resurrects the idea that birds evolved from dinosaurs —an idea that had been dormant for a century.

1980 Louis and Walter Alvarez put forward the asteroid impact theory of dinosaur extinction.

1985 Discovery by scientists of the British Antarctic Survey of the depletion of ozone in the upper atmosphere.

1988 Hottest northern hemisphere summer on record brings public awareness of global warming.

1991 Chicxulub crater in Yucatan is pinpointed as the site of the impact that may have caused the dinosaur extinction.

1992 Joe Kirschvink suggests the *snowball Earth theory*—that the Earth was covered by ice during the Precambrian.

A 50,000-year-old crater shows that the Earth is still being bombarded by meteors.

SOME WRONG DEDUCTIONS

1650 Irish Archbishop Ussher calculates date of Creation at 4004 BC. This is widely accepted.

1780 Abraham Gottlob Werner (1749–1817) theorizes that all rocks are formed in ancient oceans. He is wrong but greatly influential.

1800 Lamarck proposes a theory of evolution. It suggested that traits that are acquired in life can be passed on to the next generation. This is no longer accepted since the general acceptance of Darwin's theory of natural selection.

1862 Lord Kelvin suggests that the Earth is 20–400 million years old, based on rates of cooling.

KEY FIGURES

SIR RICHARD OWEN

Dates: 1804–92
Nationality: British
Best known for: Sir Richard Owen became the most important anatomist of his day, determining that the way an animal lived could be deduced by its shape and the organs it possessed. However, he could not quite grasp the newly developed concept of evolution.
Key discoveries: Coined the term *dinosauria* in 1842, to encompass three new animal fossils recently discovered, from which we get the name *dinosaur*.

WILLIAM BUCKLAND

Dates: 1784–1856
Nationality: British
Best known for: William Buckland was a geology lecturer at the University of Oxford. He toured Europe and established the basic principles of stratigraphic correlation and became a scientific celebrity on his discovery of *Megalosaurus*. He was the Dean of Westminster from 1845 to his death in 1857.
Key discoveries: *Megalosaurus*, the first dinosaur to be scientifically described.

WILLIAM SMITH

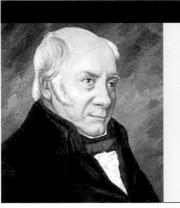

Dates: 1769–1839
Nationality: British
Best known for: William Smith observed the rocks of Britain in his role as a canal engineer, and realized that the same layers, or beds, of rocks could be traced over large areas by using their fossils to identify them. He eventually used this knowledge to compile the first ever geological map, where mainland Britain was colored according to the rock types.
Key discoveries: The principle of faunal succession, in which the same rocks can be identified by the fossils they contain, wherever they occur.

GEORGES CUVIER

Dates: 1769–1832
Nationality: French
Best known for: Georges Cuvier was one of the most influential figures in science of the time, particularly in the field of anatomy. He is regarded as the father of vertebrate palaeontology. He refused to acknowledge evolution and resisted the popularization of scientific knowledge.
Key discoveries: Classified all living and fossil things according to their similarity to one another, as we do today.

OTHNIEL CHARLES MARSH

Dates: 1831–99
Nationality: American
Best known for: Professor of palaeontology at Yale University and curator of the Peabody Museum of Natural History. He was a rival of Edward Drinker Cope, and their animosity resulted in the "bone wars," when each tried to discover more than the other.
Key discoveries: About 80 new *genera* of dinosaurs, establishing the vastness of fossil life.

CHARLES DARWIN

Dates: 1809–82
Nationality: British
Best known for: After failed attempts at careers in medicine and the church, he became a naturalist. His famous voyage on *HMS Beagle* allowed him to observe and collect examples of flora and fauna from all other the world. He built on the already existing ideas of evolution and deduced the mechanism involved.
Key discoveries: The idea of natural selection as the force that drives evolution.

EDWARD DRINKER COPE

Dates: 1840–97
Nationality: American
Best known for: Edward Drinker Cope was one of the first vertebrate palaeontologists in America and was affiliated with The Academy of Natural Sciences in Philadelphia. His arrogance drove him to fall out with Othniel Charles Marsh, instigating the "bone wars." This event stimulated the discovery of dinosaurs, but drove more methodical workers away from the science.
Key discoveries: About 65 new dinosaur *genera*.

MARY ANNING

Dates: 1799–1847
Nationality: British
Best known for: Mary Anning was a professional fossil collector, working from the beaches of Dorset and Devon in the south of England. She began work when she was 12 years old to support her family after her father died. Mary Anning is credited with finding the first complete fossil at the age of just 12 on the beach of Lyme Regis. She supplied fossils for all the eminent scientists of the day.
Key discoveries: The first full skeleton of an ichthyosaur and also of the first plesiosaur.

● See page 30–31
ICHTHYOSAURS

LOUIS SEYMOUR BAZETT LEAKEY

Dates: 1903–72
Nationality: British/Kenyan
Best known for: Louis Seymour Bazett Leakey was born in Kenya. He became an archaeologist and proved Darwin's theory that humans evolved in Africa. His most significant work was done in Olduvai Gorge in Tanzania where he found evidence of early tool use.
Key discoveries: Various species of *Australopithecus*, but given different names at the time.

CHARLES DOOLITTLE WALCOTT

Dates: 1850–1927
Nationality: American
Best known for: Walcott worked for, and became the director of, the US Geological Survey. He was a vertebrate palaeontologist and worked mostly in the Cambrian of the United Sates and Canada. He later became the Secretary of the Smithsonian Institution and was one of the most powerful figures in the American scientific community.
Key discoveries: The discovery of the Burgess Shale and its variety of fantastic Cambrian fossils.

ALFRED WEGENER

Dates: 1880–1930
Nationality: German
Best known for: Alfred Wegener was a meteorologist, doing a great deal of work in Greenland. He advocated the concept of *continental drift*, calling it *continental displacement* when he first lectured on it in 1912, although he could not think of a mechanism that would account for the phenomenon. He died in an accident on the Greenland ice cap.
Key discoveries: Proposing continental drift as a serious scientific idea.

SIR CHARLES LYELL

Dates: 1797–1875
Nationality: British
Best known for: Sir Charles Lyell was a field geologist who published a ground-breaking work *The Principles of Geology*. It explained the observed geological phenomena in terms of scientific actions rather than the works of God. He stressed that the human species must have been older than currently believed.
Key discoveries: Establishing the geological column, with time divided into periods.

PALEONTOLOGY

Fossils, the remains of life of the past, have been found just about everywhere there are deposits of sedimentary rocks. Dinosaurs, the spectacular and popular inhabitants of the past world, are a very rare part of this fossil treasure trove. Nevertheless, they have been found on all the continents of the Earth. Excavation of their remains is a very specific task carried out by experts called *paleontologists*.

DINOSAURS ALL AROUND THE WORLD

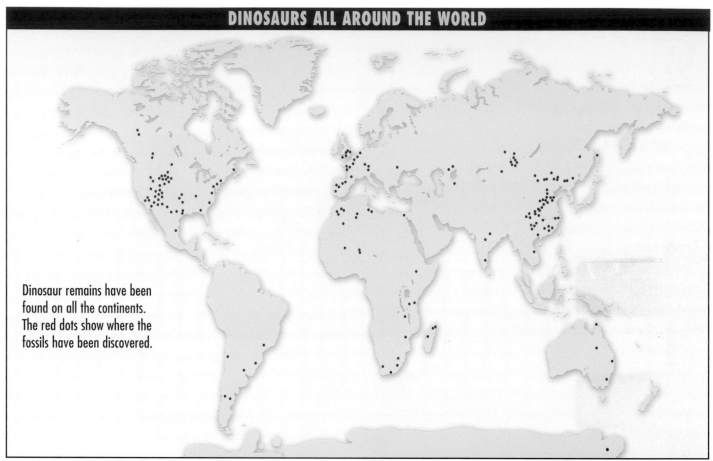

Dinosaur remains have been found on all the continents. The red dots show where the fossils have been discovered.

FINDING DINOS

Dinosaur remains are found:

- By chance — where walkers see a fossil sticking out from a cliff face, or where builders or quarry workers come across them during their work. Because of the surface of the Earth's continuous change, these exposures are common.

- By scientific expedition — where scientists investigate a certain region with exposures of the right types of rocks.

Chance exposures result from:

- Erosion by wind in the desert, where the rock is exposed and uncluttered by soil or vegetation.

- In eroded rubble where loose material has fallen from a cliff face. It may be difficult to trace the specimen back to its original bedrock.

- Where rivers have carved out gorges in the landscape.

• See pages 12-13 for more information on FOSSILS.

EXCAVATION AND TRANSPORTATION

Once found, a dinosaur skeleton is excavated using the following techniques:

- Removing the overburden: Taking off the layers of rock above it to reveal the whole thing.
- Mapping: Plotting where the individual bones lie. This is important in later study.
- Jacketing: Sealing the bones in a layer of plaster to protect them.
- Transportation back to the laboratory.

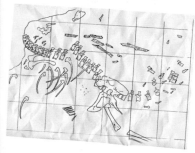

If the skeleton is for public display, it is not usually the original that is used but a cast. To create the cast, the following process is carried out:

- A mould is made of each bone of the skeleton.
- A reproduction of the bone is cast in glass fiber or some other lightweight, tough material.
- Missing bones are supplied as casts from other skeletons of the same animal.
- If there is no original material available, missing bones may be sculpted by artists.
- The skeleton is assembled on a frame, usually in a lifelike pose.

IN THE LAB

In the laboratory, specialized technicians, called *preparators*, make the specimens ready for study by the scientists. They do this by:

- Removing the plaster jacket.
- Removing any adhering matrix, the rock in which the fossil was buried, with fine tools.
- Sometimes separating the bones by dissolving the matrix in an acid bath.
- Hardening delicate bone fossils by coating them with shellac or some other varnish.

MUSEUMS WITH DINOSAUR COLLECTIONS

AFRICA
Bernard Price Institute of Paleontology, Johannesburg.
Museum of Earth Sciences, Rabat

ASIA
Museum of the Institute of Vertebrate Paleontology and Paleoanthropology, Beijing.
Academy of Sciences, Ulan-Bator.

National Science Museum, Tokyo

AUSTRALIA
Queensland Museum, Fortitude Valley, Queensland.

EUROPE
The Natural History Museum, London.
Royal Institute of Natural Sciences, Brussels.

Natural History Museum, Humboldt University, Berlin.
Palaeontological Institute, Moscow.

NORTH AMERICA
Tyrrell Museum of Paleontology, Drumheller, Alberta.
American Museum of Natural History, New York City.
National Museum of Natural

History, Smithsonian Institution, Washington, D.C.
Field Museum of Natural History, Chicago.

SOUTH AMERICA
Argentine Museum of Natural Sciences, Buenos Aires.
Museum of La Plata University, La Plata.

GLOSSARY

Algae Simple, non-flowering plants that usually grow in water.

Ammonite An extinct marine mollusc with a flat-coiled spiral shell, found as fossils mainly in Jurassic and Cretaceous deposits.

Anthracite A hard variety of coal that contains relatively pure carbon.

Archaeology The study of human history and prehistory through the excavation of sites and the analysis of physical remains.

Arthropod An invertebrate animal that has a segmented body, external skeleton, and jointed limbs.

Atmosphere The layer of enveloping gases that surrounds the Earth.

Binomial classification The classification of living things in which animals and plants are given two names, a *genus* name and a *species* name. For example *Homo sapiens* or *Tyrannosaurus rex*. This is useful when discussing various species of the same genus, such as *Homo sapiens*, *Homo erectus*, or *Homo ergaster*. Usually only the genus name, *Tyrannosaurus* or *Homo*, is used. Sometimes in a text, when the full name has already been given, then the genus name can be abbreviated to its initial, such as

T. rex. The genus name always takes a capital initial, but the species name does not, Both are written in italics.

Biped An animal that walks on two feet.

Carnivore An animal that feeds on meat.

Chert A hard, dark, opaque rock composed of silica with a microscopically fine-grained texture.

Club moss A member of a primitive group of plants, related to the ferns. Modern types are low herbaceous forms, but in the late Palaeozoic, they grew tree-sized and formed forests.

Coal A combustible black rock consisting mainly of carbonized plant matter and used as fuel.

Conifer A tree bearing cones and evergreen needle-like or scale-like leaves.

Continent Any of the world's main continuous expanses of land, usually consisting of an ancient core and surrounded by successively younger mountain ranges.

Creodont A carnivorous mammal of the early Tertiary period.

Crystal A piece of a solid substance having a natural geometrically regular form with symmetrically arranged faces.

Diagenesis The physical and chemical changes occurring during the conversion of sediment to sedimentary rock.

Eon The largest division of geological time. It comprises several eras.

Era A division of geological time, shorter than an eon but longer than a period. Typically, an era lasts for hundreds of

millions of years, and encompasses several periods. For example, the Mesozoic era comprises the Triassic, Jurassic, and Cretaceous periods.

Erosion A gradual wearing away of rocks or soil.

Eukaryote A living cell that carries its genetic material in a well-defined nucleus. Most modern living things are composed of eukaryotic cells.

Evolution The development of different kinds of living organisms from earlier forms.

Excavation The careful removal of earth from an area in order to find buried remains.

Facies A term that geologists use to cover everything about a rock or a sequence of rocks – its derivation, fossils, color, and age the landform produced—everything that makes the rock distinctive.

Fauna The animals of a particular region, habitat, or geological period.

Fern A flowerless plant that has feathery or leafy fronds.

Flora The plants of a particular region, habitat, or geological period.

Fossil The remains or impression of a prehistoric plant or animal embedded in rock and preserved.

Geology The study of the Earth, how it is made, and how it evolved.

Glaciated Covered or having been covered by glaciers or ice sheets.

Graptolite A planktonic invertebrate animal.

Herbivore An animal that only eats plants.

Hinterland The remote areas of a country, away from the coast or the banks of major rivers.

Hominid The group of animals to which human beings belong.

Ice Age A period of time when climates were cooler than they are now and glaciers were more extensive.

Ichthyosaur One of a group of swimming reptiles from the Mesozoic. They had streamlined fish-like bodies and tail fins.

Igneous Rock solidified from lava or magma.

Isthmus A narrow strip of land with sea on either side, linking two larger areas of land.

Landmass A continent or other large body of land.

Latitude The angular distance of a place north or south of the equator.

Lava Hot molten or semi-fluid rock erupted from a volcano or fissure, or solid rock resulting from this cooling.

Magma Hot fluid or semi-fluid material within the Earth's crust from which lava and other igneous rock is formed by cooling.

Marginocephalians A group of dinosaurs with armored heads. They consisted of the pachycephalosaurids, like *Stygimoloch*, and the ceratopsians, like *Triceratops*.

Mass extinction An event that brings about the extinction of a large number of animals and plants. There have been about five mass extinctions in the history of life on Earth.

Metamorphic Rock that has undergone transformation by heat, pressure, or other natural processes without actually melting.

Meteorite A piece of rock from space.

Mineral A naturally-formed inorganic substance with a specific chemical composition. Minerals are the building bricks of rocks.

Molecule A group of atoms bonded together.

Mosasaur A member of a group of big swimming reptiles of the Cretaceous period, closely related to modern monitor lizards.

Mucus A slimy substance secreted by the mucus membranes and glands of animals for lubrication and protection.

Omnivore An animal that eats both plants and meat

Organ A structure in a living body that carries out a particular function. Organs are made up of tissues.

Organism An individual animal, plant, or single-celled life form.

Paleo- As a pretix, this means *something ancient.*

Paleontology The study of ancient life and fossils.

Peat Partly decomposed vegetable matter forming a deposit on acidic, boggy ground. It is dried for use in gardening and as fuel.

Period A division of geological time that can be defined by the types of animals or plants that existed then. Typically, a period lasts for tens of millions of years, and is further subdivided into sub-periods, called *epochs,*

then subepochs, and finally stages.

Petrify To change organic matter into stone by encrusting or replacing its original substance with a mineral deposit.

Phenomenon A fact or situation that is observed to exist or happen, especially the existence of something that is in question.

Plankton The tiny animal and plant life that drifts in the waters of the ocean.

Plate tectonics The process whereby the surface of the Earth is continually being created and destroyed—new material being formed along ocean ridges and old material being lost down ocean trenches. The movement involved causes the continents to travel over the Earth's surface.

Plesiosaur A large fossil marine reptile of the Mesozoic era, with large, paddle-like limbs and a long flexible neck.

Pliosaur A plesiosaur with a short neck, large head and massive toothed jaws.

Pterosaur One of a group of flying reptiles from the Mesozoic. They flew with leathery wings supported by an elongate finger, *Pterodactylus* was a pterosaur.

Radioactivity The process in which an atom of a particular element breaks down to form another element. This process is accompanied by a release of energy which is the basis of nuclear power.

Reef A ridge on the sea bed giving rise to shallow water. Most reefs are formed from the remains of living creatures.

Rift valley A steep-sided valley formed by subsidence of the Earth's surface between nearly parallel faults.

Rock A naturally formed inorganic substance that makes up the Earth. A typical rock will be made of several types of mineral.

Silica A hard, unreactive, colorless compound that occurs as quartz and as the principal constituent of sandstone and other rocks.

Salinity The amount of salt dissolved in sea water.

Sediment Matter carried by water or wind and deposited on the land surface or seabed.

Sedimentary Rock that has formed from sediment deposited by water or wind.

Sedimentology The aspect of geology that deals with the deposition of sand and silt and other sediments before becoming sedimentary rocks.

Seismic Of or relating to earthquakes or other vibrations of the Earth and its crust.

Shingle A mass of small rounded pebbles, especially on a seashore.

Stratigraphy The aspect of geology that deals with the sequence of deposition of rocks, their structures and fossils, and interprets them to find out about conditions of former times.

Taphonomy The study of what happens to a dead organism before it becomes a fossil.

Tectonics Large-scale processes affecting the structure of the Earth's crust.

Thyreophorans A group of dinosaurs that carried armor. They consisted of the plated stegosaurs, such as *Stegosaurus*, and the armored ankylosaurs, such as *Euoplocephalus.*

Tissue The living substance of a body. Tissue is made up of cells and is the substance from which organs are built.

Trilobite A segmented arthropod, common in Palaeozoic seas.

Vertebrate An animal with a backbone.

Volcano A mountain or hill having a crater or vent through which lava, rock fragments, hot vapor, and gas are or have been erupted from the Earth's crust.

INDEX

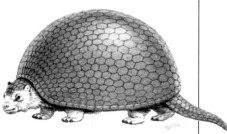